SCIENTIFIC PRINCIPLES
AND METHODS
OF STRENGTH FITNESS

SECOND EDITION

SCIENTIFIC PRINCIPLES AND METHODS OF STRENGTH FITNESS

SECOND EDITION

John Patrick O'Shea, Ed.D.

Oregon State University

Random House New York

Cover by Baseball Magazine, Sha Ltd., Tokyo

Second Edition
9876543

ISBN: 0-394-34892-3

Manufactured in the United States of America

preface

The objective of this book has been to provide a meaningful understanding of the principles and methods of acquiring strength fitness without delving too deeply into the intricacies of exercise physiology. Thus, this book is designed to provide the fundamental knowledge and techniques that are essential in developing a lifelong, quality strength-fitness program for those with a limited background in exercise physiology.

In the past decade continuing research in the field of exercise physiology has significantly altered our conceptual approach to developing strength fitness. Consequently, large portions of the book were completely rewritten with even a shift in emphasis on the subject matter. In revising the subject matter, an attempt was made to utilize fundamental exercise physiology as a tool to build a better understanding of the mechanisms upon which the elements of strength fitness depend. Therefore, the reader will find two new chapters, two chapters consolidated, and the remainder of the book extensively rewritten. Chapter 1 is rewritten and expanded to provide a greater depth in strength physiology. Chapter 2 presents a survey of the basic research in strength development. Chapters 4, 5, 6, and 7 have been updated with more contemporary methods and techniques of strength-fitness training for athletes and students. Chapter 8 offers new theories on the causes of muscle strains and outlines flexibility exercises that are helpful in preventing strains. Finally, Chapter 9 (which was exceedingly challenging to rewrite) provides a stimulating approach to strength fitness for middle age. A large portion of the material in this chapter is based upon the author's personal experiences as a middle-aged jogger, cyclist, mountain climber, and weightlifter.

A great debt of gratitude is paid to my wife Susie, Dick Irvin, Leonard Kauffman, and Don Campbell for reviewing the text and providing constructive criticism. A special thanks also to Mrs. Dorothy Seida for her secretarial service. I am particularly grateful to Miss Toni Smith for her special help in the final preparation of the manuscript.

Corvallis, Oregon   J.P.O'S.
January 1976

contents

dynamics of
strength fitness

The purpose of this chapter is to provide a meaningful framework of the chemical and mechanical processes related to muscle function without delving too deeply into its intricacies. Only by understanding the processes by which muscles adapt to the type, intensity, and duration of training can strength-fitness programs be designed intelligently.

STRENGTH FITNESS

Strength fitness, as used in this book, is the physiological function of the skeletal muscles, their ability to exert force (dynamic or static strength), to repeat contractions (endurance), to contract in proper sequence with other muscles or muscle groups (coordination), and to allow mobility of body joint action (flexibility). Any deficiency in strength fitness will be related to one or more of these components. Deficiencies can be corrected, but only within certain limits. The limits depend upon two factors: the biological quality of the individual's muscular system as related to the four components; and the type, quality, and duration of the training program designed to correct the deficiency.

SAID AND PROGRESSIVE OVERLOAD PRINCIPLES

There are two fundamental physiological concepts which are central to the acquisition of maximum strength fitness. First, all efficient and effective strength-training programs are based upon the SAID principle (Specific Adaptation to Imposed Demands). This principle tells us that the training demands must be specific in order to obtain the desired effects. The concept is referred to as "specificity of training." That is, strength training is for increasing strength, and endurance training is for increasing endurance. Furthermore, the SAID principle says that in order for one to realize maximum training effects, the imposed demands must be of a magnitude to force adaptation by the body. The imposed demands, however, must be gradually intensified over an extended period of time, otherwise the components of strength fitness will not develop to their maximum functional potential. Thus evolves the second vital training concept, the Progressive Overload principle. Application of this principle ensures that the systems of the body will be subjected to training stresses of continuously increasing magnitude.

Therefore, the training programs presented in the chapters of this book focus on the application of the SAID and Progressive Overload principles as they apply to pushing the systems of the body to maximum dynamic strength, endurance, and flexibility.

THE MUSCULAR SYSTEM

The muscular system, by means of contractions and relaxations, produces the movements of the body as a whole and as parts. Working closely with the muscles are tendons, fasciae, and aponeuroses, all of which secure the ends of the muscles and determine the direction of their pull.

Types of Muscular Tissue. On the basis of structure and function, muscle tissue is classified into three types: smooth, cardiac, and striated (see Fig. 1.1).

Smooth muscle tissue, also known as "nonstriated muscle," constitutes the involuntary muscles. Smooth muscle tissue is found in the wall of the digestive tract, the trachea and bronchi, the urinary bladder and gallbladder, the urinary and genital ducts, the walls of blood vessels, the capsule of the spleen, and the iris of the eye. The action of smooth muscles is not subject to voluntary control but is involuntary.

Cardiac muscle tissue, heart muscle, is found only in the heart. Heart action is involuntary, automatic, and rhythmic. Heart muscle responds to the progressive overload principle in much the same manner as skeletal muscle. At both submaximal and maximal work loads, a trained heart, when compared to an untrained heart, has a lower work rate and a larger stroke volume. Aerobic-type exercise improves cardiac efficiency which is essential in developing maximum strength fitness.

Striated muscle tissue, also called "striped muscle," characterizes the skeletal or voluntary muscles. Striated muscle tissue comprises all muscles attached to the skeleton. They are under voluntary control. Approximately 700 skeletal muscles comprise the muscular system. The skeletal muscles can function separately but they are grouped into units for effective movement. In initiating and executing a movement, whole groups of muscles are involved, working as teams. Muscles are arranged in opposing or antagonistic groups: flexors and extensors, adductors and abduc-

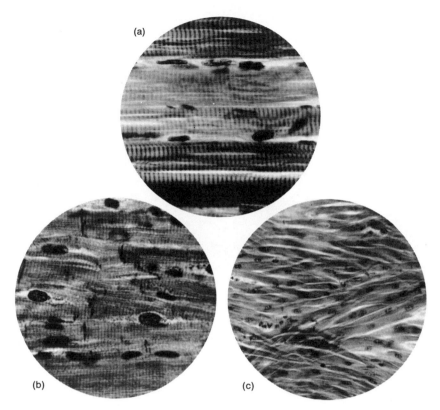

Fig. 1.1 The three kinds of muscle as they appear under the light microscope. Skeletal (a) and cardiac (b) muscle are made up of long, multinucleate fibers. Smooth muscle (c) is made up of single, spindle-shaped cells. (Skeletal muscle courtesy of Ward's Natural Science Establishment, Inc. Others, courtesy of TURTOX/CAMBOSCO, Macmillan Science Co., Inc., Chicago, Ill.)

tors, internal rotators and external rotators. For example, when a person wants to bend his arm, he flexes the muscles of the upper arm; that is, he makes them contract. The antagonist muscles (triceps) in this case are the extensors of the upper arm; they relax and elongate, thus permitting the arm to bend.

Definition of muscular and joint movements

Technical terms describe the various roles which a muscle assumes during physical activity. Some of these terms, defined below and illustrated in Fig. 1.2, are not definitive, and the reader may wish to consult a variety of textbooks for broader interpretations.

Prime mover: the muscle that bears the principal responsibility for a specific joint action.

Synergist: any muscle which contributes to a definite action, but cannot be classified as a prime mover.

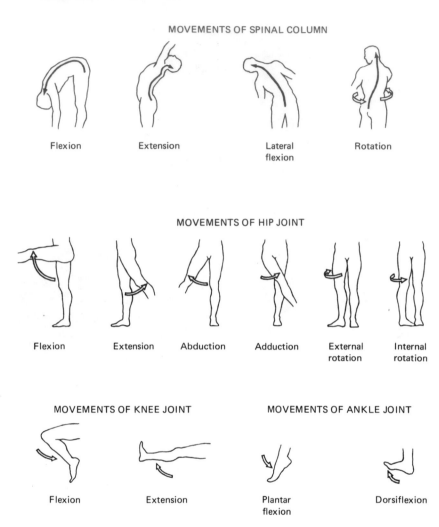

MOVEMENTS OF SPINAL COLUMN

Flexion   Extension   Lateral   Rotation
                                    flexion

MOVEMENTS OF HIP JOINT

Flexion   Extension   Abduction   Adduction   External   Internal
                                                  rotation   rotation

MOVEMENTS OF KNEE JOINT   **MOVEMENTS OF ANKLE JOINT**

Flexion   Extension   Plantar   Dorsiflexion
                                    flexion

Fig. 1.2 Muscular and joint movements from *Strength, Power and Muscular Endurance for Runners and Hurdlers* by John Jesse (Pasadena, California: The Athletic Press, 1971).

Assistant mover: a muscle which aids the prime mover to effect joint action.

Stabilizer: a muscle which anchors, steadies, or supports a bone or body part so that another active muscle may have a firm base upon which to contract.

Neutralizer: a muscle which contracts to counteract or neutralize an undersized action of another contracting muscle.

Using the various actions of the arm as an example, we will illustrate the following definitions of muscle and joint movement.

Flexion: the decreasing of the angle between two segments of the body, as illustrated by bending the arm at the elbow.

Extension: the increasing of the angle between two segments of the body; for example, the arm, as it goes into extension, becomes straight.

Abduction: the movement of a part of the body away from the midline of the body. The arm, in abduction, is raised.

Adduction: the opposite of abduction. The raised arm is moved down toward the midline of the body.

Rotation: the movement of a part of the body turning on its longitudinal axis. The arm, our example, joins the palm of the hand in illustrating this motion; the palm turns on its longitudinal axis and turns upward with the forearm in supination or downward in pronation.

Hyperextension: extreme extension of a limb or part of the body. The arm is hyperextended beyond the straight line formed by normal extension.

The above definitions are illustrated by the muscle functions involved in the two-hand curl exercise (see p. 48). This exercise begins from a standing position; with the arms fully extended, the weight is then curled to the chest. As the weight is lifted, the prime movers, the biceps, come into play. Then the assistant movers, the radial flexors of the forearms, are activated. Next the stabilizers, the latissimus dorsi, form a strong base for the biceps to perform their function by holding the upper arm firm during adduction and extension, thus preventing the entire shoulder from pulling forward. Finally, the posterior deltoid acts as the neutralizer by counteracting the shoulder flexion action of the biceps.

Skeletal muscle structure

Skeletal muscle is composed of long, multinucleated cylindrical fibers of varying length. The contractible structure of a muscle fiber is made up of long thin elements called myofibrils. Myofibrils exhibit alternating light and dark bands, which give the fiber its striated appearance. The striations arise from a repeating variation in the density, or concentration, of protein along the myofibrils.

Each myofibril is surrounded by a thin sheath of connective tissue called the endomysium. A bundle of fibers held together by a sheath of connective tissue forms a fasciculus. Finally, large numbers of faciculi enclosed by a heavier sheath of connective tissue form a muscle (see Fig. 1.3).

An electrically polarized membrane surrounds each fiber. When the membrane is temporarily depolarized, the muscle fiber contracts; it is

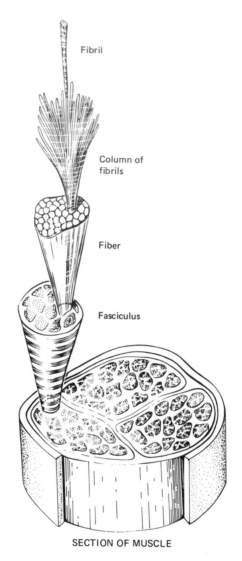

Fibril

Column of
fibrils

Fiber

Fasciculus

SECTION OF MUSCLE

Fig. 1.3 Construction of a section of muscle to show the relationship of its individual parts to the whole. An individual muscle fiber contains many fibrils, and a fasciculus contains many muscle fibers. A muscle is a composite of many fasciculi. Adapted from Sigmund Grollman's *The Human Body,* 2nd ed., © 1969, Macmillan Publishing Company, Inc.

by this means that the activity of muscle is controlled by the nervous system.

All the muscle fibers, innervated by a single motor nerve fiber from the spinal cord, are called a motor unit. A single motor nerve fiber may supply anywhere from 1 to 150 or more muscle fibers. Within a single muscle, tremendous variation exists in both the size and the number of muscle fibers, so that one motor unit may be as much as 50 times as strong as another. An impulse traveling down a motor nerve is transmitted to the muscle membrane at the motor "end plate"; then a wave of depolarization sweeps down the muscle fiber causing a single twitch. The summation or adding together of individual muscle twitches leads to strong and concerted muscle movements. As the number of contracting motor units increases, the force of a contraction increases proportionally. The strength of contraction increases as more and more motor units are stimulated. A muscle contraction continues until the stimulation stops, or the muscle becomes fatigued; that is, when the energy supplies to the muscles or within the fibers become depleted. Muscle relaxation normally occurs when the nerve stimulation stops.

The All-or-None Principle (with respect to skeletal muscle). To understand how muscles contract, we must discriminate carefully between the contraction of a whole muscle and the contraction of its individual fibers. Although a whole muscle cannot contract maximally, a single fiber of it can respond only maximally, *or not at all.* Upon receiving a stimulus from the motor reserve fiber the individual muscle fiber contracts completely or not at all. However, the contraction force that results from excitement of a muscle can vary, depending on the contractile state of the fiber when it is stimulated. If appropriate nutrients are available and a muscle is warm and not fatigued, the contraction is strong. On the other hand, if primary nutrients are not available and the muscle is fatigued, a weak contraction results.

Types of skeletal muscle contraction

The following terminology defines the physiology of various types of muscle contractions.

Isometric (static). A muscle contraction is isometric when the length of muscle does not shorten during contraction. Tension develops, heat is produced but no mechanical work is performed.

Isotonic (dynamic). A muscle contraction is isotonic when the muscle is able to contract, shorten or lengthen, and work is performed. Both concentric and eccentric contractions are isotonic.

Concentric. In a concentric contraction a muscle develops tension sufficient to overcome resistance so that the muscle fiber actually shortens and moves a body segment in spite of the resistance.

Eccentric. An eccentric contraction with given resistance overcomes the muscle tension so that the muscle actually lengthens.

During muscular activity, muscle contraction is a mixture of both isometric and isotonic movement. For example, in executing a deep-knee bend (see p. 56) with a load, in the down phase the hip and thigh extensors must develop sufficient tension to modify both the load held on the shoulders and the gravitational force, to lower the body to the squat position at a reasonable controlled speed. The down phase is an eccentric contraction of the hips and thighs which acts as a brake against the load and the pull of gravity. Otherwise, the lifter would end up crushed against the floor by the load. In the recovery phase from a deep-squat position, hip and thigh extensions are involved. Therefore, the hip and thigh extensors must contract concentrically, overcoming the force of gravity, to perform the movement.

At the same time isotonic contraction is taking place in the hips and thighs, isometric muscle contraction is occurring in the back muscles. Throughout the deep-knee bend movement the back muscles serve as synergists. That is, they contribute to the execution of the movement while in a fixed contracted position. This prevents the upper body from bending at the hip joint while resisting the force of the load being held across the upper back and shoulders.

Factors Determining Force of Muscle Contraction.   The magnitude of the contractible force of muscle depends upon a number of factors which deserve attention.

Natural endowment.   Individuals who have been endowed with parents or close relatives possessing great physical strength may inherit this physical characteristic. Training, however, will improve muscular strength at any given level.

Size of muscle.   A positive relationship exists between the cross-section of a muscle and its potential maximum contractible force. A skeletal muscle can exert a tension of about 4–6 kilos for each square centimeter of its cross-section. This does not mean that individuals with large muscles will be stronger than those with smaller ones. It means that hypertrophy (increase in size) of muscle through training will increase its potential contractible force.

Number of contracting fibers.   A direct relationship exists between the recruitment of motor units and the strength of muscle contraction. The greater the number of motor units recruited, the greater the strength of contraction. High intensity training over a prolonged period of time improves the ability of the neuromuscular system to recruit greater numbers of motor units, and hence a greater number of muscle fibers, to contract under given conditions.

Work load.   If there is no load to work against, a muscle contracts extremely rapidly. The average muscle achieves a state of full contraction in approximately one-twentieth of a second. When the work load is increased to equal the maximum force that the muscle can exert, the velocity of contracture becomes zero and no contraction takes place (isometric contraction).

Length of muscle at the time of contraction. Skeletal muscle is normally under slight tension when attached by its tendons to the bones. Under this condition it is moderately stretched (its resting length). When a muscle is at its normal resting length and receives an impulse to contract, it contracts with the maximum force of contraction for the existing conditions. Shortening a resting muscle to less than its normal fully stretched length reduces the maximum tension of contraction. The potential force of contraction reaches zero when the muscle has shortened to approximately 60 percent of its maximum resting length.

Lever system. The principle function of the bones, in making body movements, is to act as levers. Muscles supply the force to move the bones. It is the relationship of the muscle insertions around a joint that results in the lever system. A difference exists in the force a muscle is able to create within itself, and the same force acting through the leverage system. For example:

a. if the muscle force is great but the leverage is poor at the joint, the actual load lifted may not be great;

b. if the muscle force is poor but the leverage is good, the results are the same.

Physiological state of the muscles at the time of contraction. If the number of nutrients available for contraction is reduced or if the muscle is fatigued, the number of fibers contracting within a muscle is reduced. Nerve impulses will continue, but contractions will become weaker and weaker because of the depletion of energy supplies in the muscle fibers themselves.

Composition of muscle tissue

Skeletal muscle is approximately 75 percent water, 20 percent protein, and 5 percent inorganic and organic material, and nonprotein nitrogenous substances.

Muscle proteins. Myosin, which is the most abundant protein in muscle, forms the fibrils. It plays an important role in the contraction of the fiber when it combines with adenosine triphosphate (ATP). Actin is the second protein of the muscle fibril and it, too, plays a major role in contraction of the fiber. Together, myosin and actin combine to form actomyosin. The breakdown of the ATP actomyosin linkage, as a result of ionic upset when a volley of motor nerve impulses reaches the muscle, provides the energy necessary for muscle contraction. (See Table 1.1.)

Red and white muscle fibers. Skeletal muscle fibers, when chemically analyzed, are found to contain different quantities of myoglobin. Myoglobin is a protein substance that is chemically related to hemoglobin.

TABLE 1.1   Chemical Changes During Muscle Contraction

As a result of ionic upset (calcium upset):

a) Adenosine Triphosphate (ATP) $\rightleftarrows$ Adenosine Diphosphate (ADP) + Phosphoric Acid + Energy for Contraction

   (oxygen is not required here — anaerobic)

b) Phosphocreatine $\rightleftarrows$ Creatine + Phosphoric Acid + Energy

   (oxygen is not required here — anaerobic)

   The energy liberated here is provided from glycogen oxidation and is used for the actual shortening of the muscle fiber.

c) Glycogen $\rightleftarrows$ Lactic Acid + Energy*

   Provides the energy necessary for the resynthesis of ATP.

   (nonoxidative synthesis of ATP — aerobic)

d) $\frac{1}{5}$ Lactic Acid + Oxygen $\rightarrow$ Carbon Dioxide (CO_2) + Water (H_2O) + Energy (aerobic)

   In the presence of oxygen $\frac{1}{5}$ of the lactic acid is oxidized in the mitochondria to carbon dioxide and water, and the energy released is used to oxidize the remaining $\frac{4}{5}$ of lactic acid into glycogen by the liver. This process is referred to as a "steady state": O_2 uptake = O_2 consumption. If sufficient oxygen is not available (oxygen debt) lactic acid accumulates which interferes with muscle contraction.

---

* The energy liberated in the breakdown of glycogen is not responsible for the contraction energy, since muscle will still contract as long as phosphocreatine and ATP are present. In the breakdown of glycogen the energy released is used for the synthesis of phosphocreatine from creatine and phosphoric acid.

Like hemoglobin, it possesses an affinity for oxygen. Myofibers that contain a high content of myoglobin, and thus oxygen, are referred to as red or fast-moving muscle fibers. Those that contain lesser quantities of myoglobin are called white or slow-moving muscle fibers. Red fibers are rich in capillaries, mitochondria, lipids, and oxidative enzymes. The white fibers show higher levels of adenosine triphosphate, creatine phosphate and glycolytic enzymes, while capillaries and mitochondrial densities are lower than red fibers.

Due to their high oxygen affinity, red muscles are capable of greater endurance. Large quantities of red fibers are found in muscles such as the antigravity skeletal muscles (trunk and leg extensors, cardiac muscle, and the diaphragm). Within red muscles there exist relative degrees of redness. Endurance athletes possess a preponderance of red muscle fibers. White fibers are generally found in flexor muscles and are characterized by the speed of contraction and by the magnitude of exerted tension. Using a muscle needle and a biopsy technique, researchers found that weightlifters had twice as great an area of white fibers versus red fibers as runners or untrained subjects had. This scientific evidence supports the SAID concept. Physical training, within limitations, can alter the ratio of red and white fibers (see Chapter 2).

Inorganic compounds. Potassium, magnesium, sodium, phosphorous, and calcium are the inorganic compounds or principal minerals that play a vital role in muscle function.

Organic compounds. Glucose and glycogen constitute the major organic compounds of muscle tissue. Glucose is a simple sugar formed from the breakdown of carbohydrates during the digestive process. It is transported by the blood to the muscles where it eventually supplies energy for cellular metabolism. When glucose is not required immediately it is stored in the muscle cells as glycogen. The amount of glycogen stored in muscle cells is sufficient to supply the muscle's needs for a few minutes or a few hours, depending upon the type of activity. Additional glucose is converted into fat which also can be used later for body energy needs.

Nonprotein nitrogenous compounds. Adenosine triphosphate (ATP), creatine, phosphocreatine, and urea are the nonprotein nitrogenous compounds of muscle tissue. ATP is one of the most important compounds in muscle. It is the energy released by the breakdown of ATP that is used for the contraction of muscle (see Table 1.1). The energy liberated in the breakdown of glycogen is not involved in the contraction energy but is used in the synthesis of phosphocreatine from creatine and phosphoric acid. Oxygen is required for the combustion of glycogen and in several other phases of energy metabolism within the muscle.

Oxygen demands. In order to carry out the demands placed on it, the body requires an adequate supply of oxygen. At rest, the body requires 200 to 300 cc of oxygen per minute. In strenuous exertion, this need may be multiplied over 20 times. For emergency use, the blood and the lungs contain a small reserve of oxygen, total amounts being 1800 cc in the blood and 2250 cc in the lungs.

Training improves the body's capacity to deliver and utilize oxygen by increasing (a) lung ventilation (more air is processed by the lungs), (b) oxygen-carrying capacity of the blood (there is greater passage of oxygen into the blood), (c) the capacity of the heart to pump more oxygen-rich blood to the muscle tissue and remove waste products (carbon dioxide), (d) muscle tissue capillary density with a resulting increase in movement of oxygen within the tissue mass where oxygen consumption takes place, and (e) muscle mitochondria content. The basic process of oxygen movement is physical diffusion between capillary blood and mitochondria.

Chemical changes during muscle contraction

Once the muscle fiber receives the action potential to contract, a series of chemical changes take place in the fiber. The muscle receives its energy to contract from the combustion of carbohydrate; in the final step of this process, oxygen is consumed and carbon dioxide (CO_2) and water (H_2O) produced.

In Table 1.1, the initial chemical phase involved in the contractile cycle (stages a and b) is "anaerobic." This means that the energy necessary for contraction can be supplied without the presence of oxygen. However, the second phase of the contractile cycle (stages c and d) is "aerobic" and takes place only in the presence of oxygen.

Heat production. Most of the fuel that is consumed in a muscle contraction is expended as heat. Approximately 30 percent of the energy is converted into mechanical work; the rest is freed as heat, which is employed to maintain body temperature.

Anaerobic Contraction and Oxygen Debt. During the initial phase of muscle contraction oxygen is not required. This is referred to as the nonoxidative or anaerobic phase. Energy for contraction is released through a series of enzymatic reactions. The anaerobic process is extremely important, since it enables a person to engage in a variety of strenuous physical activities of short duration and high intensity, such as sprint running. During this type of anaerobic activity the role of ATP utilization greatly exceeds the rate of muscle oxygen consumption, resulting in "oxygen debt." Oxygen debt is reflected in a production and accumulation of lactic acid, an end product of muscle contraction. Excessive amounts of lactic acid halt muscle contraction by inhibiting release of the necessary energy for the synthesis of glycogen. In large quantities, this substance causes muscle pains and symptoms of muscle fatigue. When high intensity exercise stops, oxygen consumption is greater so that the body can oxidize and remove the lactic acid. This high postexercise level of oxygen consumption continues until the oxygen debt is repaid.

Anaerobic training. This type of training includes two categories:

1. exercise so short and severe that the cardiovascular-respiratory system cannot meet the oxygen demands of the working muscle, for example, sprint running;

2. exercise that, though severe in some instances, is voluntarily cut short before a steady state is reached, for example, weightlifting.

Circulatory-respiratory System and Aerobic Power. An efficient cardiovascular system is essential for the attainment of a high level of aerobic power and muscular endurance, both of which involve the use of stored fuel (glycogen), generally oxidized in the process of releasing energy.

Because oxygen stores in the body are minimal, oxygen must be continuously supplied by the blood circulation, if the oxidative processes are to proceed during aerobic activity. In general then, for the development of muscular endurance, a highly functioning circulatory-respiratory system is necessary. This premise is justifiable when considering two processes which are central to the development of endurance.

The first process involves the diffusion of oxygen from the gas phase into the blood and diffusion of carbon dioxide from the blood into the gas phase. To increase the efficiency of this process, development of alveolar hyperplasia is important. This means that the alveolar capsules are opened to provide a greater surface for the passage of gases between the lungs and the blood during aerobic activity. The second process, cardiac output, is related to the first process and involves the total volume of blood expelled by the heart per minute. Increased cardiac output in turn increases the quantity of bood available to the working muscle tissue. Muscle cells thus have the opportunity to extract greater amounts of oxygen from the blood and to expell the waste products of exercise, permitting a reduction of the accumulation of lactic acid. The reduction of lactic acid decreases fatigue for the endurance athlete.

Other prime factors involved in muscular endurance are increases in blood volume and hemoglobin concentrate in the red blood cells and in growth of the muscle capillary beds. All of these factors combined are critical in achieving maximum muscular endurance and aerobic power.

Aerobic training. Aerobic training is submaximal activity that develops the circulatory-respiratory system, such as long-distance running, cycling, cross-country skiing, and swimming. At the start of aerobic training an oxygen debt will ooour as a result of the initial anaerobic muscle contraction. Soon, however, the continued exercise permits the cardiovascular system to meet the oxygen demand and a "steady state" is established. In a steady state, respiration, heart rate, and lactic acid production reach, and are maintained at, a relatively high balanced level. Oxygen consumption equals oxygen uptake. In reality, however, at any exercise level above the anaerobic threshold, you are doing "nonsteady state" exercise, which means you cannot keep it up indefinitely.

This brief discussion of the circulatory-respiratory processes and aerobic training holds specific implications for the strength athlete (hammer-thrower, shot-putter and Olympic lifter) striving to attain maximum strength fitness. By now it should be clear that conventional weightlifting is not an aerobic training activity. Due to the nature of weightlifting, short bursts of energy followed by rest with no requirements for a continuous high-energy state, it is classified as an anacrobic training activity. Generally speaking, weightlifting contributes little or nothing to the development of aerobic power. There is, however, one method of weightlifting that does tax the cardiovascular system and develops muscular endurance and a limited level of aerobic power, and this is "aerobic weight training" (see Chapter 4).

TABLE 1.2 Primary Effects of Aerobic and Strength Training

Aerobic training		Strength training
Increase In:		*Increase In:*
O₂ uptake		Size of muscle fibers
Capillary structure and function of heart and lungs		Strength of muscle contraction

Cardiac output
  Stroke volume
  Heart rate–decrease
	METABOLISM
	Nutrition
		Strength of bones and ligaments

O₂ carrying capacity of blood	Proteins Fats	Capillary density of muscle

Circulation:
  in the delivery of nutrients to the cell and removal of the waste products of exercise and metabolism
	Carbohydrates
	Vitamins
	Minerals
	
	Fuel utilization
		Flexibility
		
		Neuromuscular function
		  Speed of muscle contraction

Dimension of the capillary tissue system Cell metabolism O₂ uptake at cell level	Energy release	Coordination

Olympic lifting and power lifting of high intensity, while not stressing the cardiovascular system sufficiently to increase aerobic power, do create an increase in the nutritional and waste disposal demands of muscle tissue. Therefore, the aerobically fit strength athlete is more likely to provide his muscle with an adequate supply of energy and have quick disposal of the waste products of exercise. Any increase in the nutritional and energy need of the muscle cells, however, must be met by a corresponding increase in the flow of blood through the capillary beds of the skeletal muscle. It is in this circulatory process that aerobic training plays a vital role in the total development of a strength athlete. (For a comparison of aerobic and anaerobic training effects see Table 1.2.) Theoretically, the strength athlete in a relatively high state of aerobic fitness will recover more rapidly between strenuous workouts and consequently be able to train at or near maximum capacity with greater frequency. Relative aerobic fitness for the strength athlete means the ability to run the mile and a half aerobic fitness test fast enough to be rated in the good category (see Chapter 9).

SPECIAL FEATURES OF MUSCLES

Muscle hypertrophy. Muscle hypertrophy is an increase in size of the muscle as a direct result of forceful muscular training. As a consequence of such training the diameters of the individual muscle fibers increase, with the fibers gaining in total quantity of contractile myofibrils as well as in various nutrients and intermediary metabolic substances such as ATP, phosphocreatine, and glycogen.

Submaximal muscular training, even when sustained over a prolonged time period, does not result in significant hypertrophy. Only forceful muscular training will cause hypertrophy even though the training might occur for a relatively few minutes each day. Muscle hypertrophy occurs, then, as a direct result of the application of the SAID and progressive overload principles. In weightlifting, for example, the muscles hypertrophy to a degree directly related to the intensity of the work loads to which they are subjected. Also, the degree of hypertrophy that can be expected from training is to some extent controlled by the biological makeup of an individual's muscle system. This may explain why some people, while they may increase their strength through weightlifting, realize very little measurable growth in muscle size.

Muscle atrophy. Muscle atrophy is the opposite of muscular hypertrophy; it results when the muscle is used for very weak contractions. Usually, atrophic muscle responds to training loads of 30 percent or less of what is considered normal strength for a given age and sex. The term atrophy is relative since different strength limits exist for each muscle group according to the type and respective intensity the training program places on the body systems.

Dynamic strength. Dynamic strength is the ability of a muscle or muscle group to exert force in a given situation and involves the phenomenon of inertia. That is, the weight or object being lifted or moved must be first accelerated, and once a velocity has been attained, the weight or object has momentum that causes it to continue moving even after the contraction is over.

Dynamic strength is achieved only through the application of the SAID and progressive overload principles. Submaximal muscle training does not result in maximum development of strength. For example, 1–3 repetitions using 90 percent or better of a person's 1-RM (one repetition maximum) will effect a maximum increase in strength, while 10 repetitions using sixty percent of 1-RM will have a greater effect on muscular endurance and hypertrophy. Evidence of this can be seen in the bodybuilder possessing the Mr. America type of physique. Mr. America, in comparison to an Olympic lifter, exhibits the ultimate in muscle hypertrophy brought about by an intense training program of high repetitions with relatively low resistance. The Olympic lifter on the other hand, while exhibiting comparatively less muscular hypertrophy than his Mr. America counterpart, develops a far higher level of dynamic strength as a result of training at a high intensity with heavy resistance for 1–3 repetitions. This comparison presents a good example of "specificity of training" and illustrates too an important point: while weightlifting may result in an increase in muscular hypertrophy, it does not necessarily follow that there will always be a corresponding increase in dynamic strength.

Dynamic muscle endurance.   Muscle endurance is the capacity of the skeletal muscles to perform work of moderate intensity for prolonged periods of time. The capacity for muscular endurance is determined by (1) the blood flow to the muscles, (2) the strength of the muscles, (3) the work load being used in relation to maximum effort, (4) the length and frequency of contraction (the greater the frequency of dynamic contraction the higher the energy consumption), (5) the length of the rest intervals between contractions, and (6) the physiological state of the muscle cells during exercise (their ability to resynthesize the nutrients necessary for muscle contraction). Mr. America is a good illustration, too, of an athlete possessing a high degree of dynamic muscular endurance. His weight-training program of high-repetitions–low-resistance is specifically designed to elicit the maximum in muscular hypertrophy and, hence, is almost totally endurance-oriented.

Muscle fatigue.   Fatigue is the inability of the contractile and metabolic processes of muscle fibers to continue supporting a set work rate. Exercise physiologists do not agree upon the physiological site of fatigue, nor do they really distinguish between fatigue and muscle impairment. There is general agreement, however, that the limiting factors in muscle contraction are found at the cellular level and may include changes in the chemical properties of the muscle fibers, breakdown of the ATP–ADP system, depletion of the glycogen stores, or an inability to remove the end products (lactic acid) of contraction due to oxygen deprivation. These factors are the primary contributors to the fatigued state of muscle in the endurance athlete. The total effect is a loss of the muscle's ability to relax and the inevitable development of a state of contracture (muscle cramps).

   Muscle fatigue in the strength athlete is perhaps more complicated and may be associated with a chain of chemical events which block the calcium ion regulated action potential essential for efficient electrical control of the mechanical contractile process of the muscle fiber. This upsets the synchronization of motor unit firing, resulting in an overall loss of muscle contractility. Since strength of contraction depends almost entirely upon selective motor unit recruitment, this would explain why a strength-trained muscle fatigues faster than an endurance-trained or an even weaker muscle.

Flexibility.   One of the main components of strength fitness, flexibility, is the elasticity of tendons. Flexibility allows uninhibited joint motion and perfection of movement which in turn provides a margin of safety to the joint at its surrounding connective tissue structure during physical activity. Flexible tendons, compared to inflexible tendons, are resistant to strain. (See Chapter 8 for flexibility exercises.)

Coordination.   Coordination is the properly timed contraction and decontraction (relaxation) of the prime muscle movers and their antagonistics as they produce movement. Muscle coordination is controlled through the central nervous system which connects the function of the muscle groups to incoming stimuli from organs governing equilibrium, vision, state of contraction of other muscles, etc. Conditioned reflexes, the ready responses to correct movement patterns that an athlete develops by repetition of the same movement over and over again, is coordination. Coordination is improved by developing flexibility or strength if either of these qualities is lacking. At the same time, poor coordination may result from relative overdevelopment of strength or flexibility in one group of muscles.

Threshold of training

The percent of maximum work load required in training to elicit a continual increase in performance rises with increasing muscle strength or aerobic power to a point where the training stimulus becomes ineffective. This is the "strength limit" or "aerobic power limit." For example, the training stimulus required to elicit an increase for a maximum bench press by 5 percent a month for six months grows steeper each month. Finally in the last two months the lifter may find it impossible to improve his maximum performance; his training stimulus is so high it finally becomes ineffective. The "LAW OF DIMINISHING RETURNS" is involved which means that the training stimulus is approaching the point of zero return (see Chapter 7, The K-Value System of Determining Training Loads).

Speed of Increase in Strength. The speed of increase and the limits of muscular strength and aerobic power are determined by the intensity and duration of training. An increase in strength is greater the more the initial strength differs from the maximum strength limit. Initial rapid strength gains from weight training may be attributed to an increased recruitment of motor units and not an increase in muscle size (hypertrophy). Increased motor-unit summation is characteristic among experienced strength athletes who over a prolonged period of training continue to increase their strength without increasing muscle size (see Chapter 5).

Gains in dynamic strength may be measured by using the following formula:

$$VP_0 = \frac{100\%}{week}\left(\frac{P_t}{P_0} - 1\right)\left(\frac{0}{0}/week\right),$$

where

P_0 = the initial strength,
P_t = strength at the time of test,
V = the speed of increase in strength.

Example. $VP_0 = \frac{100\%}{5}\left(\frac{100}{50} - 1\right)\left(\frac{0}{0}/week\right)$

$VP_0 = 1$ or 100% increase in 5 weeks
or 20% per week for each week.

In this example, the athlete could lift 50 pounds at the beginning of the five-week training period and 100 pounds at the end. This represents a 100 percent increase for the five weeks or 20 percent for each week.

Muscle force

Force is the effect one body has upon another. A weight can be lifted only when force has been applied; however, it is possible to have force without motion, as when gripping the bar tightly before lifting (isometric contraction). Force does not affect motion when its result is zero though the effects can be seen and measured in terms of magnitude, direction, and point of application.

In Olympic lifting, for example, we are mainly concerned with the use of force for changing the "state of motion" of the lifter and the weight. Internally, the lifter obtains his force through the contraction of his muscle fibers. The magnitude of muscle force generated is in direct proportion to (a) the size and number of fibers contracting, and (b) the speed at which active fibers are forced to lengthen (eccentric contraction). Force is inversely proportional to the speed with which fibers shorten (concentric contraction). This means the heavier the load is to be lifted, the greater the muscle force will be required to move it and the slower the fibers will contract. Or, the lighter the load is, the less force will be required and the faster the fibers will contract.

Newton's Laws of Motion. The whole science of force is based upon three fundamental laws known as Newton's Laws of Motion. Simply stated they are:

1. Every body continues in its state of rest or uniform motion in a straight line except insofar as it is compelled by forces to change that state.

    This is also known as the Law of Inertia (the Latin for idleness or laziness). In more simple terms, the Law of Inertia says that everything in the universe is at rest. Force is necessary to initiate motion, and once something is in motion, further force must be applied to slow down, stop, speed up, or change direction.

    Thus, the weightlifter, to get a weight moving (as in snatching) must first overcome its "inertia" and then keep the weight moving until the lift is completed.

2. The acceleration of a body is proportional to the forces causing it.

    In effect, Newton's second law says that a greater force is required to reach a certain speed in a given time if one starts from a stationary position than if one is already in motion. Applied to Olympic lifting (snatching or cleaning), the momentum of the bar during the second pull will be dependent upon the magnitude and direction of the first pull. Thus, the first pull must be strong and as fast as body leverage will permit.

3. For every action there is an equal and opposite reaction.

The effect upon one body is known as the action and that upon the other the reaction. For example, in snatching the lifter applies force to lift the weight (the action), and at the same time he is pushing against the floor (reaction) with a force equal to that which moves the weight upward.

Related to Newton's laws of motion and their application to weight-lifting are the principles relating to levers both within the body and out-side.

Lever system.   While the force of muscle contraction will be dependent upon the seven factors discussed earlier, the actual load lifted by the lifter depends on the leverage system of the skeleton. In weightlifting, one must keep in mind that a difference exists in the force a muscle is able to generate within itself and the force acting through a leverage system. For instance, in snatching, poor technique would prevent a lifter from assuming a body position which would provide maximum pulling leverage and hence would reduce the effectiveness of the generated muscle force.

The human body acts predominantly through third-class levers such as the elbow joint. Three factors present in a lever system are *R* (the load or resistance), *F* (the muscle force), and *A* (the axis).

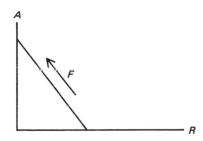

The elbow joint and bicep muscle as a third class lever.

In weightlifting, the force necessary to lift a weight *(R)* can be de-termined by the following formula:

$$F = \frac{R \times RA}{FA},$$

where

F = force of contraction,

R = load or resistance,

RA = length of resistance arm; distance
    from load *(R)* to axis *(A)*,

FA = length of force arm; distance from
    force *(F)* to axis *(A)*,

using the following values: $R = 40$ lbs, $RA = 1$ft, $FA = .16$ ft.

$$F = \frac{R \times RA}{FA} = \frac{40 \times 1}{.16}$$

$$= 250 \text{ lbs}$$

By increasing the FA to .20 ft a more favorable leverage can be achieved. This illustrates the advantage a lifter has who possesses good leverage in the arms, back and legs.

$$F = \frac{40 \times 1}{.20}$$

$$= 200 \text{ lbs.}$$

Fifty pounds less force is needed by the biceps to lift 40 pounds when the FA is increased.

Muscle power. Power, the rate at which work is done, is represented by the following formula:

$$P = \frac{\text{WORK}}{\text{TIME}}$$

In any given time the more work that is done, the greater the power. Power is measured in terms of foot-pounds per second or horsepower (1 horsepower = 550 foot-pounds per second). For example, a lifter who deadlifts 500 pounds to a height of $2\frac{1}{2}$ feet in 2 seconds produces the following horsepower:

$500 \times 2\frac{1}{2} = 1250$ foot-pounds of work,

$$\frac{1250}{2} = 625 \text{ foot-pounds of work each second,}$$

or at the rate of

$$\frac{625}{550} \quad \text{or} \quad 1.13 \text{ h.p.}$$

Athletes in general, and especially Olympic weightlifters, must strive to develop power through a full range of movement. The athlete's ability to exert maximum muscular power is dependent upon his flexibility, neuromuscular coordination, and a competitive attitude encompassing determination and concentration.

MEASURING MUSCLE STRENGTH

Measuring and evaluating muscle strength serves several useful purposes: to determine strength, endurance, and fatigue differences between isometric, concentric, and eccentric muscle contraction, and to reveal deficiencies in muscle function. Obtaining valid strength measurements is

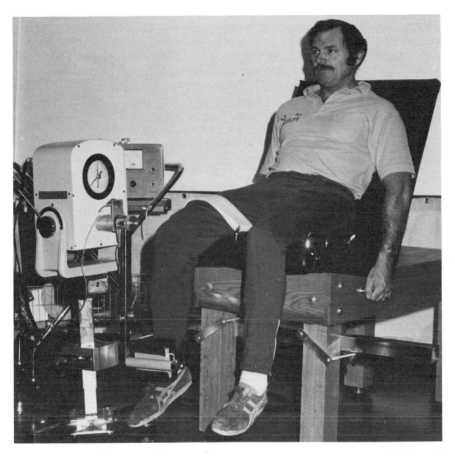

Fig. 1.4 Cybex II dynamometer which measures muscle force both isometrically and isotonically.

dependent upon the reliability of the testing instrument used and upon the subject providing maximum voluntary muscle contraction for the given conditions. Testing instruments are simple spring scales, cable tensiometers, and the more sophisticated Cybex II dynamometer (see Fig. 1.4), an isokinetic device that measures muscle force both isometrically and isotonically. In testing strength isotonically the Cybex measures muscle force at a set velocity in both extension and flexion in degrees per second. The velocity can be varied from zero degrees per second (isometric contraction) to 210 degrees per second to measure fast moving strength and muscular endurance. The force generated by the muscles at a set velocity is recorded on a moving chart from which muscle power is determined. Knowing the velocity of muscle contraction we can determine the power (force × velocity = power).

Maximum dynamic strength of large muscle groups (shoulders, arms or legs) may be determined without the use of sophisticated measuring devices by performing one repetition maximum (1-RM) in one or more weightlifting movements, such as the bench press and squat. For assessing a combined level of muscular strength and endurance 5–8 RMs are recommended and for muscular endurance only 12–15 RMs. One major limitation to attempting to measure isotonic strength through weightlifting exercises is that the subject must know the tecnniques of the test lift and this requires a pretraining period prior to testing. Assessing dynamic strength is a complicated function but it provides a useful evaluation of overall functional strength which isometric measurement does not.

Electromyographic (EMG) measurement of muscular strength. Electromyograms make it possible to study the relationship between muscle stimulation and the amount of force developed, the type of muscle contraction (concentric versus eccentric), and the effects of fatigue.

Each time a muscle fiber is stimulated a small portion of electrical current spreads away from the muscle to the skin. This electrical potential may be very great at the skin if many muscle fibers contract simultaneously. By placing two electrodes on the skin or inserting electrodes into the muscle, an electrical recording called the electromyogram can be made when the muscle is stimulated. As the muscle contracts the electrical discharges are picked up and magnified greatly by the EMG which then uses them to cause a pen to vibrate over a moving chart paper. The width of each pen vibration depends upon the number of muscle fibers being stimulated, and the frequency with which the pen vibrates indicates how often the fibers are being stimulated.

SUMMARY

This chapter has presented an overview of the primary physiological principles and concepts related to the acquisition of dynamic strength fitness. Strength fitness as used in this book is described as being the strength of muscle contraction, muscular endurance, flexibility, and coordination. Key concepts central to the development of strength fitness are the SAID and progressive overload principles. The composition, size, and function of muscle tissue is dependent upon the type, intensity, and duration of training one engages in. The training program too, must be specific. That is, strength training for strength, endurance training for muscular endurance, and aerobic training for cardiovascular-respiratory endurance. Unless one is a strength athlete whose primary goal is maximum strength, one should follow a training program that develops a balanced level of both strength fitness and aerobic power.

SELECTED BIBLIOGRAPHY

Astrand, O., and Kaare Rodahl. *Textbook of Work Physiology.* New York: McGraw-Hill Book Co., 1970.

Best, C. H., and N. B. Taylor. *The Living Body,* 4th ed. New York: Henry Holt & Co., 1958.

Clark, H. H., and David H. Clark. *Developmental and Adapted Physical Education.* Englewood Cliffs, N. J.: Prentice-Hall, Inc., 1963.

Dyson, G. *The Mechanics of Athetics.* New York: Dover Publications, Inc., 1971.

Guyton, A. C. *Textbook of Medical Physiology,* 4th ed. Philadelphia: W. B. Saunders Co., 1971.

Johnson, W. R., ed. *Science and Medicine of Exercise and Sports,* 2nd ed. New York: Harper and Brothers, 1974.

Karpovich, P. V. *Physiology of Muscular Activity.* Philadelphia: W. B. Saunders Co., 1965.

Kraus, H. *Therapeutic Exercise,* 2nd ed. Springfield, Ill.: Charles C Thomas Publisher, 1963.

Pernow, B., and B. Salten, eds. *Muscle Metabolism During Exercise.* New York: Plenum Press, 1971.

Poortmans, J. R., ed. *Biochemistry of Exercise.* Baltimore: University Park Press, 1969.

Rasch, P. J., and R. K. Burke. *Kinesiology and Applied Anatomy.* Philadelphia: Lea & Febiger, 1959.

Shephard, R. J., ed. *Frontiers of Fitness.* Springfield, Ill.: Charles C Thomas Publishers, 1971.

Articles

Berger, Richard A. "Comparison of the effect of various weight training loads on strength." *Research Quarterly* **36**:141 (1965).

Brouha, L., and B. M. Savage. "Variability of physiological measurements in normal young men at rest and during muscular work." *Rev. Canad. Biol.* **4**:131–143 (1945).

Brouha, L., "Training," in W. R. Johnson, ed. *Science and Medicine of Exercise on Sports.* New York: Harper and Brothers, 1960.

Capen, Edward K. "The effects on systematic weight training on power strength and endurance." *Research Quarterly* **21**:83–9 (1950).

Chui, Edward. "The effect of systematic weight training on athletic power." *Research Quarterly* **21**:188–94 (1950).

Darcus, H. D., and N. Salter. "The effect of repeated muscular exertion on muscle strength." *Journal of Physiology* **129**:325–36 (1955).

Muller, E. A. "Training muscle strength." *Ergonomics* **2**:216–223 (1959).

Muller, E. A. "Physiology of muscle training." *Rev. Canad. Biol.* **21**:303–313 (1962).

Orban, W. A. R. "Dynamometer strength test and performance of weightlifters in international competition." *Journal of Sport Medicine* **2**:12–16 (1962).

research in
strength development

Since the end of World War II, a vast amount of experimental work has been carried out by researchers seeking the answers to the phenomenon of muscle strength and function. The results of their research have pushed back the frontiers of knowledge concerning strength fitness by producing new scientific training concepts. Consequently, trial and error approaches to strength development should be a thing of the past. Today's generation of coaches, athletes and students of strength fitness have at their disposal a large amount of scientific and technical information necessary for designing quality, result-producing training programs.

DYNAMIC STRENGTH TRAINING

Research studies by DeLorme [1] indicate that for the development of strength, 1–3 repetitions for 3–4 sets with maximum load are best; and for muscular endurance, 10–12 repetitions for 3–4 sets with maximum load are best. Studies by Berger [2] and O'Shea [3] indicate that for developing a combination of strength and muscular endurance, the most effective progressive weight training program is 5–6 repetitions, 3–4 sets, with maximum or near maximum loads (90 percent or better). Through the practice of progressive resistance exercise, DeLorme and his co-workers produced an increase in the circumference and strength of the arms and thighs. To build power and induce muscle hypertrophy, DeLorme used a system of heavy-resistance–low-repetition exercise. He describes power as the whole potential strength of a muscle used over a short period of time (as in weightlifting) and endurance as the ability to use a muscle against moderate or light resistance for long periods (as in circuit training). DeLorme recommends a system of heavy-resistance–low-repetition exercise to build up power and volume in muscle groups and low-resistance–high-repetition exercise to develop endurance. The DeLorme technique of training is to start with a light weight for a given number of repetitions and progressively increase the load from one-quarter to one-half to three-quarters and then maximum load for the given number of repetitions and sets. His system is used by the majority of competitive lifters and weight training coaches today.

Zinovieff [4] believed that DeLorme's technique was too fatiguing and that too great a strain was placed on the muscles. Using a modified form of DeLorme's system, Zinovieff developed the "Oxford technique." The Oxford technique retains the principle of heavy resistance and low repetitions but reverses the procedure of DeLorme by starting with (after a brief warmup) the heaviest weight first and progressively decreasing the load.

McMorris and Elkins [5] made a study comparing the DeLorme and Oxford techniques; they reported that a 5.5 percent increase in strength resulted from the Oxford technique. They believed, however, that a series of experiments is necessary before one can conclude that these methods produce consistently different results.

MacQueen [6], in a survey among competitive lifters and body builders, found that there is a distinction between the type of exercise used to develop muscular hypertrophy and that used to develop strength. In the hypertrophy program, muscle groups were exercised on alternative days, 8–10 repetitions, 3–4 sets; the weight used was the maximum that the trainee could handle for the given number of repetitions and sets. In the power program the initial weight was never less than the maximum that could be lifted in 2–3 repetitions, 4–5 sets. The power program is essentially one of decreasing the number of repetitions while increasing the load.

Norbert Schemansky [7], former world and Olympic champion, based his training on DeLorme's technique with a few variations. Training five days per week, he worked with maximum or near maximum weights for 1–3 repetitions, 3–5 sets, at least twice a week.

ISOMETRIC TRAINING: ITS EFFECTS
ON DYNAMIC STRENGTH

The effectiveness of isometric training in the improvement of dynamic strength has been and continues to be scientifically controversial. Beyer [8] advocated the position that isometric training does not benefit dynamic strength, nor does dynamic strength benefit isometric training. Dynamometer strength-testing by Orban [9] and Johnson and O'Shea [10] have proven to be poor indicators of dynamic-strength performance. On the other hand, Asmussen et al. [11] found a correlation of $r = 0.8$ between isometric and dynamic strength. This contradictory evidence may be accounted for in several ways. Singh and Karpovich [12] reported that, when testing isometric and dynamic strength, maximal forces were developed in different lifting positions. They also found that isolated muscle force can only be measured isometrically while work and power through dynamic testing are not measuring the same things. Isometric strength is not dynamic strength (i.e., strength in action).

ISOMETRIC-ISOTONIC TRAINING: THEIR EFFECTS ON LIMB SPEED

Increasing the strength of a muscle involved in a specific movement will result in an increase in speed of the movement. This theory is sub-stantiated by researchers who have investigated the effects of increased strength on limb speed [13, 14, 15, 16] and have clearly established that significant increases in strength are associated with significant increases in speed of movement. Smith [15], using a combination of isometric-isotonic weight programs, found a strength increase of 17 percent asso-ciated with a speed increase of 8 percent. In a similar experiment, Smith and Whitley [16] found a strength increase of 22 percent associated with a 6 percent speed increase. Chui's study [13] disclosed that a significant gain in limb strength, resulting from isometric and dynamic weight train-ing exercises in a specific range of movement, was accompanied by significant gains in speed of the same movement. In another study, Smith and Whitley [17] compared the effects of three different training programs on strength and speed of limb movement. The two groups, training on isometric-isotonic and dynamic overload, recorded significant speed and strength increases. No significant speed or strength gains were registered by the free-swing control group.

Contrary to the evidence presented on strength and speed, some in-vestigators have concluded there is little relationship between the two. It is their view that speed of movement is not increased by isometric training until strength becomes a factor in overcoming any resistance. This theory is supported by Tucker [18] who found that isometric training increased strength but had no effect on maximal power, acceleration, or velocity of either resisted or free horizontal movements. Swegan [19] has reported that isometric training resulted in a significant loss of speed in flexion and extension of both the elbow and knee.

From the evidence available it seems that further investigation is needed in the relationship of isometric training and the development of speed. All that can be stated at this time is that dynamic strength train-ing seems to be superior in increasing limb speed movement.

RELATIONSHIPS OF MUSCULAR STRENGTH TO ENDURANCE

One of the interesting strength fitness questions is the relationship be-tween dynamic strength and dynamic muscular endurance. Berger [20] and Shaver [21] have measured this relationship through assessment of the bench press movement. Both researchers measured dynamic strength as 1-RM. Relative dynamic strength endurance, however, was measured differently in the two studies. Berger assessed it as the number of times a load, which was 50 percent of maximum dynamic, could be lifted by each subject. Shaver used the number of times an individually determined load, representing 75 percent of each subject's dynamic strength, could be lifted as relative dynamic endurance. At the same time, Shaver also studied the absolute endurance of his subjects in terms of the number of times a common load of 75 percent of the groups' mean maximum dynamic strength could be lifted.

In both investigations a negative correlation between maximum dynamic strength and relative dynamic endurance was found (Berger, −0.40 and Shaver, −0.19). Shaver, though, in comparing dynamic strength to the absolute dynamic endurance of a common groups' mean performance of 75 percent, found a positive correlation of 0.93.

To summarize the findings of Berger and Shaver, it seems that while maximum dynamic strength is a factor in dynamic endurance, it is by no means a good indicator of the latter. For example, in comparing muscular endurance levels between lifters A and B, with 1-RM in the bench press of 400 and 200 pounds respectively, both are given 50 percent of their 1-RM and asked to perform a maximum all out effort in repetitions, lifter B would in all probability execute the most bench presses. This is a good indication that a training increase in dynamic strength does not result in a proportional increase in dynamic endurance.

BIOCHEMICAL RESEARCH IN MUSCLE DEVELOPMENT

While research physiology has greatly contributed to the advancement of training methods for the development of dynamic strength and muscular endurance, future advances are found in the area of muscle biochemistry. The study of the adaptive changes in the exercised skeletal muscle requires intensive investigation; that is, the study of the muscle enzyme system, the magnitude, regulation, and interaction of energy stores, uptake and oxidation of energy-rich compounds during exercise, and the role of the endocrine system.

Skeletal muscle response to training.   Biochemical research in the past decade has shown that there is an increase in the functional capacity of skeletal muscle in response to weight training and repetitive exercise. Such an increase is a reflection of changes in the structure of muscle fiber and in its protein content.

Muscle fibers.   Morpurgo [22] in the late 1800s was the first to demonstrate that muscle hypertrophy could be achieved through exercise. Goldspink [23], in studying mice, found that prior to a weight training program small muscle fibers outnumbered large fibers. Following the weight training program, mouse biceps hypertrophied in a specific manner, that is, large fibers outnumbered small fibers. This suggests a shift in fiber type—small fibers converting to large fibers. In studying the conversion of white fibers to red fibers Barnard, Edgerton, and Peter [24] verified that treadmill running results in a drop in the percentage of white fibers and an increase in the percentage of red fibers in both white and red areas of guinea pig gastrocnemius.

Muscle capillaries. Carrow, Brown, and VanHuss [25] evaluated the number of capillaries per fiber and fiber size after subjecting rats to a program of forced swimming. In red fibers the increase in the number of capillaries per fiber was one-fifth the increase in muscle size. The capillaries per fiber and fiber size increased in a 1 to 1 ratio in white fibers. Thus, white fibers developed a greater increase in vascularity than did red fibers under the same conditions.

Muscle mitochondria. Gollnick and King [26] and Kraus [27] found an increase in the number and size of mitochondria in rats following a training program of forced running and swimming respectively. Kiessling, Piehl, and Lundquist [28] placed subjects on a running program of 28 weeks which doubled the pretraining number of mitochondria but produced no change in their size. Electron microscope and biochemical studies have revealed that both the size and the content of muscle mitochondria increase due to endurance activities [29, 30].

Muscle proteins. Gordon, Kowalski, and Fritts [31] found that low-intensity–prolonged-duration exercise, such as swimming and free wheel-running, increased the concentration of sarcoplasmic protein, whereas the high-intensity–short-duration exercise (weightlifting) elevated the content of myofibrillar (actomyosin) proteins in the quadriceps muscle of the adult rat. That is, swimming increased the endurance capacity of the muscles, and weightlifting strengthened the contactile function. Additional evidence augmenting the theory that muscle proteins change in composition as a result of training is offered by Jaweed et al. [32]. They found that a six-week exercise program of free wheel-running and weightlifting produced a significant change in the structural proteins (sarcoplasmic and myofibrillar proteins) of female rats. The specific changes in protein functions may be considered adaptive changes to a specific quality of stress. High-intensity–short-duration activity necessitates strong and enlarged contractile units. The stimulus that induces the myofibrillar hypertrophy seems to be the intensity of the workload on individual fibers [32]. While weightlifting appears to increase contractile proteins, Goldspink [23] cautions that such an increase may not be entirely desirable. He reasons that an increase in myofibrillar protein without an associated increase in mitochondria may dilute the supply of energy and thus diminish muscle endurance.

In summary, changes in contractile, sarcoplasmic, and mitochondrial proteins resulting from training suggest: (1) alterations in muscle proteins are related to the type, intensity, and duration of exercise; (2) that changes in muscle proteins partially explain improved strength or endurance following specific anaerobic or aerobic training; (3) that red and white muscle fibers are not unalterable; and (4) that the SAID principle (see Chapter 1) is a valid concept when applied to muscle tissue that is subjected to a training stress.

Anabolic steroid. Anabolic steroids have been used widely throughout the international athletic world since the 1964 Olympic Games. In recent times, the use of anabolic steroid agents by athletes for the purposes of improving dynamic strength has been the subject of intense medical controversy.

Present day anabolic steroid agents are synthetic derivatives of testosterone, the male hormone produced in the Leydig cells of the testes. Anabolic agents have been medically used for some time in the treatment of osteoporosis, fracture healing, severe burns, muscular dystrophy, and for building protein tissue. The anabolic action of these drugs (their ability to increase protein biosynthesis in skeletal muscle) has been the primary reason for their widespread use by athletes, especially strength athletes.

The practice of administering anabolic steroid to athletes has been condemned by the medical profession and outlawed by the International Olympic Committee on the grounds that the drugs are a threat to the health of the athlete and also that no scientific proof exists to substantiate claims of their significantly benefiting strength development.

The American Medical Association (AMA) has pointed out the potential danger involved in anabolic steroid administration: steroids may result in adrenal and testicular shutdown, acute liver problems, prostatic hypertrophy, and excessive fluid retention. While the arguments advanced by the AMA opposing the use of steroid agents contain much validity, current research conflicts in many respects with the AMA's stated position. Examination of the research literature indicates that under controlled conditions, present-day synthetic anabolic steroids effectively increase protein biosynthesis in muscle tissue and enhance dynamic strength when accompanied by a severe weight training program [33, 34, 35, 36, 37, 38]. This same research uncovered no adverse physiological or biochemical effects.

The question, however, of whether anabolic steroids exert a positive effect on the acquisition of dynamic muscle strength still remains open for scientific inquiry. Contradictory evidence presented by other investigators [39, 40, 41, 42] may be attributed to differences in drugs or dosage, treatment duration, diet, training intensity, or biochemical variability of subjects.

Steroid studies that produced significant increases in dynamic strength had several common denominators: (1) diets of the subjects were supplemented with a high protein supplement, and (2) the strength training involved was based upon the progressive overload principle.

Some investigators [40, 41] have questioned the need of supplementing the diets of subjects on an anabolic steroid program. In the biochemical progress of developing dynamic muscle strength, however, increasing nitrogen retention seems to be a critical factor. O'Shea [43] found in a steroid study involving competitive swimmers in which a protein supplement was not fed that no change in body weight or performance occurred. In a subsequent study, where a protein supplement was included, a significant increase in body weight and nitrogen retention was produced [34]. In this study lean body tissue was not assayed. However, since the subjects were competitive athletes in hard training, one might believe that the gain in body weight was not due to the accumulation of adipose tissue or water retention. The work of Ward [37] supports this belief. Celijowa and Homa [44] found Olympic weightlifters often are in negative nitrogen balance, and hence an anabolic steroid and a protein supplement would be valuable in preventing the loss of lean muscle. As a result of his work, Torizuka [45] believes that anabolic steroid not only inhibits catabolism but also directly accelerates protein synthesis. This is highly desirable in strength building. Additional support is presented by Albanese [46] who demonstrated that anabolic steroid induced a significant and consistent improvement in protein utilization in almost all of 50 subjects.

Utilizing the Steroid Protein Activity Index developed by Albanese [46], O'Shea and Winkler [34] have quantitatively measured the anabolic potency of steroid agents on protein metabolism in swimmers and weightlifters and found a beneficial effect. The *SPAI* is found in the equation:

$$SPAI = \frac{NBSP}{NISP} - \frac{NBCP}{NICP} \times 100$$

where

$NBSP$ = nitrogen balance in steroid period,
$NISP$ = nitrogen intake in steroid period,
$NBCP$ = nitrogen balance in control period,
$NICP$ = nitrogen intake in control period.

The *SPAI* permits the examination of the protein metabolism effects of steroids under conditions of self-selected food intake. *SPAI* measures the effects of steroid agents on protein metabolism more systematically in terms of nitrogen balance to nitrogen intake ratios, rather than in terms of nitrogen output or balance per se [46]. In other words, it gives a quantitative measure of the efficiency of anabolic steroids on protein metabolism.

The use of the *SPAI* affords the advantage of compensating for changes in nitrogen intake which may be induced by the steroid. The magnitude of the *SPAI* value is in direct proportion to the metabolic effects of the steroid agent. The *SPAI* provides a means of estimating, rather than guessing, the dosage ranges of anabolic steroid which could be expected to offset the protein-catabolic effects of prolonged intensive physical training and of meeting the demand for increased protein biosynthesis in muscle tissue. Theoretically, by creating a positive *SPAI* ratio, the athlete should be able to recover more rapidly between strenuous workouts and to train at capacity or near capacity with greater frequency. As the quality of workouts improve, so will strength and performance.

In the final analysis, assessment of the research literature does not permit one to make the specific statement that anabolic steroid agents are completely safe and can or should be administered to athletes of any age. Furthermore, long-term clinical evaluation is still necessary.

REFERENCES

1. DeLorme, T. L., and A. L. Watkins. "Techniques of progressive resistance exercise." *Archives of Physical Medicine* **29**:263 (1948).

2. Berger, Richard A. "Comparison between resistance load and strength improvement." *Research Quarterly* **33**:637 (1962).

3. O'Shea, John P. "The development of strength and muscle hypertrophy through selected weight programs." *Research Quarterly* **37**:95–107 (1966).

4. Zinovieff, A. N. "Heavy-resistance exercise, the Oxford technique." *British Journal of Physical Medicine* **14**:129 (1951).

5. McMorris, R. O., and E. C. Elkins. "A study of production and evaluation of muscular hypertrophy." *Archives of Physical Medicine* **35**:420–26 (1954).

6. MacQueen, I. J. "Recent advances in the technique of progressive resistance exercise." *British Medical Journal* **11**:1193–98 (1954).

7. Personal interview by the author with Norbert Schemansky at Michigan State University's Weightlifting Clinic, March 10, 1962.

8. Beyer, R. A. "Comparison of static and dynamic strength increase." *Research Quarterly* **33**:329–333 (1962).

9. Orban, W. A. R. "Dynamometer strength test and performance of weightlifters in international competition." *Journal of Sports Medicine* **2**:12–16 (1962).

10. Johnson, L., and J. P. O'Shea, "Anabolic steroid: effects on strength development." *Science* **164**:957–959 (1969).

11. Asmussen, E. et al. "The relation between isometric and dynamic muscle strength in man." Communication from the Testing and Observation Institute of the Danish National Association for Infantile Paralysis, No. 20, Hellerup, Denmark, 1965.

12. Singh, M., and P. V. Karpovich. "Isotonic and isometric forces of forearm flexors and extensors." *Journal of Applied Physiology* **21**:1435–1437 (1966).

13. Chui, E. F. "Effects of isometric and dynamic weight training exercises upon strength and speed movement." *Research Quarterly* **35**:246–57 (1964).

14. Clark, D. H., and F. M. Henry. "Neuromotor specificity and increase speed from strength and development." *Research Quarterly* **32**:315–25 (1961).

15. Smith, L. E. "Influence of strength training on pre-tensed and free-arm speed." *Research Quarterly* **35**:554–61 (1964).

16. Smith, L. E., and L. D. Whitley. "Influence of strengthening exercise on speed of limb movement." *Archives of Physical Medicine & Rehabilitation* **46**:772–77 (1965).

17. Smith, L. E., and L. D. Whitley. "Influence of three different training programs on strength and speed of a limb movement." *Research Quarterly* **37**:132–42 (1966).

18. Tucker, R. M. "Effects of isometric strength development on speed and power of resisted and non-resisted horizontal arm flexion." Master's thesis, Pennsylvania State University, 1967.

19. Swegan, D. B. "The comparison of static contraction with standard weight training in effect on certain movement speeds and endurance." Doctoral dissertation, Pennsylvania State University, 1957.

20. Berger, R. A. "Relationship between dynamic strength and dynamic endurance." *Research Quarterly* **41**:115–116 (1970).

21. Shaver, L. G. "Maximum dynamic strength, relative dynamic endurance and their relationship." *Research Quarterly* **42**:460–465 (1971).

22. Morpurgo, B. "Ueber activitats-hypertrophic der willkurlichen muskeln." *Archiv fur Pathologische Anatomie und Physiology* (Virchows) **150**:522-554 (1897).

23. Goldspink, G. "Morphological adaptation due to growth and activity," in E. J. Briskey, R. G. Cassens, B. B. Marsh, eds., *Physiology and biochemistry of muscle as a food.* Vol. 2. Madison: University of Wisconsin Press, pp. 521–36 (1970).

24. Bernard, R. J., V. Edgerton, and J. Peter. "Effects of exercise on skeletal muscle. I. Biochemical and histochemical properties." *Journal of Applied Physiology* **28**:762–766 (1970).

25. Carrow, R. E., B. Brown, and W. VanHuss. "Fiber size and capillary to fiber ratios in skeletal muscle of exercised rats." *Anatomical Record* **159**:33–40 (1967).

26. Gollnick, P., and D. W. King. "Effects of exercise and training on mitochondria of rat skeletal muscle." *American Journal of Physiology* **216**:1502–1509 (1969).

27. Kraus, H. "Effects of Training on Skeletal Muscle," in O. A. Larson, and R. O. Malmborg, eds., *Coronary Heart Disease and Physical Fitness.* Baltimore: University Park Press, pp. 134–137 (1971).

28. Kiessling, K. H., K. Piehl, and C. G. Lundquist. "Number and Size of Skeletal Muscle Mitochondria in Trained Sedentary Men," in O. A. Larson and R. O. Malmbourg, eds., *Coronary Heart Disease and Physical Fitness.* Baltimore: University Park Press, pp. 143–148 (1971).

29. Edgerton, V. R., and G. L. Carrow. "Histochemical changes in rat skeletal muscle after exercise." *Experimental Neurology* **24**:110–123 (1969).

30. Terjung, R. L. et al. "Effects of running to exhaustion on skeletal muscle mitochondria: a biochemical study." *American Journal of Physiology* **223**:549–554 (1972).

31. Gordon, E. E., K. Kowalski, and M. Fritts. "Protein changes in quadriceps muscle of rat with repetitive exercise." *Archives of Physical Medicine and Rehabilitation* **48**:296–303 (1966).

32. Jaweed, M. J. et al. "Endurance and strengthening exercise adaptations: 1. Protein changes in skeletal muscles." *Archives of Physical Medicine and Rehabilitation* **55**:513–517 (1974).

33. Johnson, L., and J. P. O'Shea. "Anabolic steroid: effects on strength development." *Science* **164**:957–959 (1969).

34. O'Shea, J. P., and Winkler. "Biochemical and physical effects of anabolic steroid in competitive swimmers and weightlifters." *Nutrition Reports International* **2**:351–362 (1970).

35. O'Shea, J. P. "The effects of an anabolic steroid on dynamic strength levels of weightlifters." *Nutritional Reports International* **4**:363–370 (1971).

36. Johnson, L. et al. "Anabolic steroid: effects on strength, body weight, oxygen uptake and spermatogenesis upon mature males." *Medicine and Science in Sports* **4**:43–45 (1972).

37. Ward, P. "The effects of an anabolic steroid on strength and lean body mass." *Medicine and Science in Sports* **5**:277–282 (1973).

38. O'Shea, J. P. "A biochemical evaluation of the effects of Stanozolo on adrenal, liver and muscle function in humans." *Nutrition Reports International* **10**:381–388 (1974).

39. Fowler, W. M. et al. "Effects of an anabolic steroid on physical performance of young men." *Journal of Applied Physiology* **20**:1038–1040 (1965).

40. Casner, S. W., and R. G. Early. "Anabolic steroid effects on body composition in normal young men." *Journal of Sports Medicine* **11**:98–103 (1971).

41. Fahey, R., and H. Brown. "Effects of anabolic steroids plus weight training on normal males—a double blind study." *Medicine and Science in Sports* **4**:54 (1972).

42. Golding, L. A., J. E. Freydinger, and S. S. Fishel "Weight size, and strength unchanged with steroids." *The Physician and Sports Medicine* **2**:39–43 (1974).

43. O'Shea, J. P. "The effects of anabolic steroid treatment on blood chemistry profile, oxygen uptake, static strength, and performance in competitive swimmers." Doctoral dissertation, University of Utah, 1970.

44. Celojowa, I., and M. Homa. "Food intake, nitrogen and energy balance in Polish weightlifters during a training camp." *Nutrition and Metabolism* **12**:259–274 (1970).

45. Torizuka, K. "The effects of anabolic steroid upon protein metabolism studied by the isotype method." *Metabolism* **12**:11–14 (1963).

46. Albanese, A. A. "Nutritional and metabolic effects of some newer steroids III Stanozolo." *New York State Journal of Medicine* **68**:2392–2406 (1964).

principles, methods, and techniques of weight training

Weight training allows individuals, regardless of their physical capacities, to train at their own level. Whatever the level of strength fitness at which the novice begins training, his success will depend to a great extent on his own self-discipline and determination. Weight training is not a "dynamic wonder course." As a rule, it requires at least two months of continuous training before the trainee can observe significant changes in strength and general appearance. During the early stages of training, the trainee can expect to experience a period of retrogression before realizing specific improvement in strength. However, he will notice minor improvements, such as an increase in appetite and more restful sleep, even at the onset of training.

This chapter attempts to provide the basic framework around which a weight training program can be constructed. It outlines a system of progressive weight training that incorporates many of the proven research concepts discussed in Chapter 1 and 2.

PLANNING A WEIGHT TRAINING PROGRAM

Following a progressive weight training program is the only method by which established goals may be achieved. There is no other way; hit-or-miss programs lead only to failure for the trainee.

Number and Length of Workouts. Three workouts per week is the usual number recommended for beginners. As the trainee improves his level of fitness and strength, he may proceed to a four-day-per-week program, utilizing the "split routine." On the split routine, the upper body is exercised on Monday and Thursday and the lower body on Tuesday and Friday. The majority of champion lifters train five or six days a week.

For the average trainee, an adequate workout can be obtained in 50 minutes with a lot of hustle. An advanced trainee or competitive lifter will require 1½ to 2 hours, chiefly because the use of heavier weights requires more rest between exercises.

Selection and Order of Exercises. In organizing and developing a weight training program, selection of the "core" exercises is of prime concern. Core exercises—power cleans, pressing movements of all types, and squats—are the foundation of every program. They are the exercises that develop the large muscle groups of the body, as opposed to assistant exercises which work only specific isolated groups. Increased strength and body size will be realized much sooner if all the major muscle groups are exercised at every workout, for they respond to heavy training much more rapidly than do isolated groups. One of the pitfalls to avoid is concentrating on a few select exercises, such as the bench press and arm curls, while neglecting the remainder of the body; such a program will ultimately end in failure.

The exercises for a well-balanced program should include at least two core exercises for the upper body region and one for the lower body and legs. The following selection and order of exercises is recommended:

Monday	Wednesday	Friday
Bench Press	Incline Press	Same as Monday
Power Clean	Parallel Bar Dip	
Curl	Upright Row	
Lat (Latissimus) Machine	Incline Dumbbell Curl	
Full Squat	Shoulder Shrug	
Pullover	Half-Squat	
Sit-Up	Hack Squat	
Toe Raise	Back Hyperextension	

Repetitions and sets. *Repetition* refers to the number of complete and continuous executions of an exercise. A 1-RM is the maximum amount of weight that can be lifted one time. A *set* constitutes x number of repetitions of an exercise. If more than one set is performed, a short rest interval (1–2 minutes) follows each set. For example, if a trainee presses 100 pounds 10 times, he has performed 10 repetitions in 1 set. Following a short rest, he repeats the same exercise for another 10 repetitions. This constitutes the second set, and so on.

Determining starting poundages. There is no rigid formula, such as using a percentage of body weight, in establishing a starting poundage for the individual exercises. "Trial and error" based upon individual capabilities is the best method. For a beginning, it is recommended that each exercise be performed 8–12 times, with a load that permits him to perform the movement correctly. Overloading and not performing the exercise correctly will impede progress and increase the possibility of injury.

Progressive weight training

Progressive weight training is a planned system of training in which the intensity of work (the repetitions or resistance) is gradually increased. It incorporates the proven research theory of training with heavy loads (90 percent of maximum) and low repetitions (1–3) for strength, and medium to light loads (80 percent and 70 percent respectively) with higher repetitions (5–6, medium; 8–12, light) for muscular endurance.

Progressive weight training can be utilized to its greatest advantage by following a weekly schedule of "heavy-light-medium" training days. Following this type of schedule the major muscle groups, together with the specific groups, are worked to their maximum capacity a minimum of once a week. Table 3.1 illustrates the extent to which the core exercises are worked in a beginning progressive weight program.

TABLE 3.1   Progressive Weight Training Schedule (sample)

	Monday (heavy)			Wednesday (light)			Friday (medium)		
	Wt.	Reps.	Sets	Wt.	Reps.	Sets	Wt.	Reps.	Sets
Bench press	135	5–6	1	135	10–12	1	135	6–8	1
	155	5–6	1	155	8–10	1	155	5–6	1
	170	4–5	1	165	8–10	2	175	5	4
	180	3–4	1						
	190	1–3	1						
	200	1	1						
Power clean	135	5	1	135	5		135	5	
	155	4	1	155	5		155	4	
	175	3	1	175	2–3	2	175	3	
	190	3	1				185	2	2
	200	2	1						
Incline press	135–175	6–10	2–3	Same as Monday			Same as Monday		
Seated dumbbell curl	30–40	6–10	2–3	Same as Monday			Same as Monday		
Parallel bar dip	30–40	6–10	2–3	Same as Monday			Same as Monday		
Lat. machine	100	6–10	2–3	Same as Monday			Same as Monday		
Situp	25	6–10	2–3	Same as Monday			Same as Monday		
Squat	200	6–8	1	Half squat			200	8–16	1
	220	5–6	1	200	5	1	225	5–6	1
	235	4–5	1	240	5	1	240	5	1
	255	3–5	1	275	5	1	255	5	2
	265	2–4	1	300	4–5	1			
	275	1–3	1	325	3–5	1			

Beginning with each Monday's heavy workout, the maximum poundages in the core exercises are increased, five pounds for the bench press and power clean and ten pounds for the squat. In studying the sample schedule, we can see that the core exercises involving the large muscle groups employ far greater resistance than do those involving specific isolated groups. These larger groups, when worked as a whole, require this greater resistance if they are to develop to their full potential.

Note, too, that it is important to complete each exercise in the proper sequence for the required number of sets before starting the next exercise. Training haphazardly by skipping around from one exercise to another will never produce the desired results. If the trainee wishes to specialize on the legs, he may perform the squat first. But he should never start a training session by doing curls. By fatiguing the arms, the trainee will be unable to make the maximum effort in the standing press or bench press.

Training for symmetry

The primary goal of weight training is improvement of the overall levels of strength fitness; secondary to this is the development of a symmetrical physique, a physique that has been developed to its overall optimum potential (see Figs. 3.1 and 3.2). Somehow, perhaps as an attention-getting device, a few trainees lose all sense of perspective and become obsessed with the desire to develop only the parts of the body that can be most easily observed by others. In their training, they emphasize all varieties of arm and chest exercises and pretty much neglect the remaining areas of the body. The finished product of such training resembles a "physical freak." Individuals such as these, with overdeveloped arms and chest and underdeveloped shoulders and legs, impart a wrong impression of the objective of sensible weight training, both in appearance and in fitness.

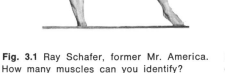

Fig. 3.1 Ray Schafer, former Mr. America. How many muscles can you identify?

Fig. 3.2 A good example of a symmetrically developed physique.

In training to obtain a symmetrically developed body, an important factor must be considered—the individual's inherited body type characteristics.* A man with a slight build has less potential to develop a heavily muscled body than a man with a larger frame, though he may develop a pleasingly trim physique.

As a guide to those seeking to achieve the potentially ideal physique, the tape measurement may be the criterion. Based on this criterion, Gri-

---

* For somatotyping, see Chapter 8.

mek [1] recommends the following method for determining the ideal proportions for each individual male:

Upper arm, muscles flexed: measure the wrist size and multiply by 2.10.

Chest: measure the wrist and multiply by 5.62.

Waist: should equal 64 percent of chest girth.

Thighs: measure the knee and multiply by 1.44.

Calves: should be 67 percent of thigh girth.

Body weight: multiply 2.55 by inches in height.

Symmetry should be everyone's goal and of particular concern to the beginner. Most beginners are faced with the problem of total underdevelopment of their bodies. This makes it essential that they follow a well-rounded training program that develops the whole body. The following are a few basic principles in training for symmetry:

1. Do not let strong points overshadow weak ones. If the legs lack size and strength, concentrate on improvement by performing an extra set or two of squats.
2. Perform the exercise in their proper sequence.
3. Work the large muscles before proceeding to isolated muscle groups.
4. Execute the exercises correctly.
5. Follow one training program for at least six weeks.

Sticking points

Following a program of progressive weight training, a human being can improve physically only so much over a period of time; if this were not so, we would all be pressing 300 pounds. A sticking point, or plateau, is reached when the trainee finds it seemingly impossible to increase the weight or repetitions during several weeks of training.

There are a number of factors involved in reaching a sticking point, and adjustment in any one or more of them may prove beneficial in overcoming it.

Overtraining or undertraining. To determine whether or not overtraining is the problem, perform one extra set in each exercise for two workouts. If, after the completion of each workout, you are completely fatigued, return to your normal workout schedule and reduce all of the exercise sets by one.

It is also possible to overtrain or undertrain only parts of the body. Many trainees, beginners and advanced, execute far too many arm and shoulder exercises and not enough leg exercises. If this is the situation, reduce all of the upper body exercises by one set and increase the leg exercises by one or even two sets. Squats can be particularly helpful in breaking a sticking point.

Improper diet.   Many times the problem of a sticking point can be traced to a poor and improper diet. The diet should be rich in complete proteins, vitamins, and minerals. Large quantities of meat, cheese, eggs, and milk must be consumed if muscle tissue is to grow. Strength cannot be improved on an average person's diet.

Mental and physical fatigue.   Constant mental or physical fatigue will result in an immediate halt in progress. Physical fatigue may be the result of insufficient rest, poor diet, or overtraining. Whichever it may be, proper adjustments can readily be made, especially in the area of rest. Each individual varies as to the amount of sleep he requires to carry out daily tasks. A person leading a physically active life may require nine hours; for the less active, six or seven are sufficient. For the weight trainee and athlete, a half-hour rest period is a great energy-booster on training days.

   An important training hint that will help in preventing sticking points is to "train in relationship to your energy output." In other words, if, at the start of a workout which is scheduled to be a maximum one, you find that the weights feel extremely heavy, substitute a light or medium workout instead. A trainee should not struggle through a maximum workout when his energy output is low. Even if he completes the workout, which is doubtful, he would risk additional fatigue or injury. If he takes it easy, his energy level will undoubtedly return to normal in a day or two, and he can train again at maximum capacity with safety.

WEIGHT TRAINING EXERCISES

Before attempting to execute any of the exercises, a trainee should carefully read the instructions concerning breathing and warm-ups.

Breathing.   Correct breathing is essential during exercise because the body requires a good oxygen supply for the muscles to do their work. Holding the breath also stabilizes the muscles of the chest, allowing the trainee to exert greater force on the weight he is lifting.

   In weightlifting, the proper technique of breathing is to inhale on the up-stroke and exhale on the down-stroke of each repetition. The most important aspect of breathing to bear in mind is that *no matter where the starting position for an exercise, inhalation takes place here.* The breath should be held until near completion of the repetition.

Warmups.   Today there exists a great amount of controversy over the physiological benefits of warming up before training or competition. Until more scientific data are obtained, it will remain the accepted practice to continue warming up. Based on the author's own experience, formal warmups and, to a lesser degree, general warmups, are necessary.

   General warmups consist of exercising the large muscle groups of the body, while formal warmups are practicing the skill involved in the activity. There is an overlapping between the two; however, through experience, individuals will develop a pattern of warming up best suited to their needs.

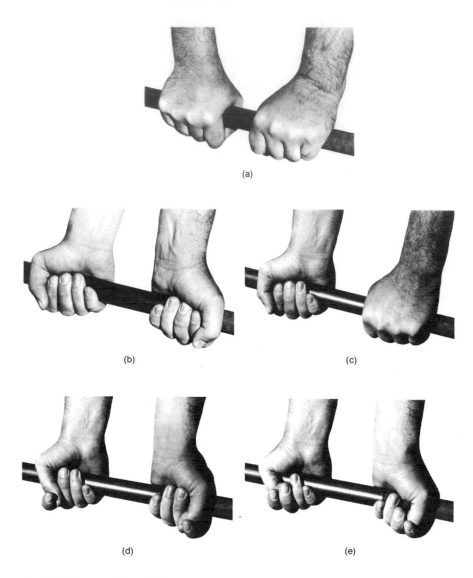

Fig. 3.3 Grips used in weightlifting: (a) pronated; (b) supinated; (c) alternating, for heavy dead lifting; (d) thumb-locking, for Olympic lifting; (e) a variation of thumb-locking, also for Olympic lifting. (d and e must be used in a supinated position in Olympic lifting.)

Presented on the following pages are 32 of the most widely known weight training exercises, which are practiced universally by both beginning and advanced weight men. Each exercise lists the major muscles involved in the movement. The prime mover is indicated by the abbreviation "P.M." and the assistant mover by "Asst." Instructions for the starting position and execution of the movement are clearly stated. Learn the correct technique of each exercise by practicing first with a very light weight. This will save time in the long run by preventing injuries and the acquisition of incorrect lifting techniques which are hard to overcome. Do the exercises correctly without cheating so that the muscles which are the prime movers in a particular movement have the opportunity to do their work. Consult Figs. 3.46 and 3.47, at the end of the chapter, for locations of the muscles involved.

The first two exercises, the dead lift and power clean, are the basic lead-up exercises to all overhead lifting movement and should be learned during the first training session. The five hand grips illustrated in Fig. 3.3 should be studied carefully before any lifting is attempted.

UPPER-BODY EXERCISES

1. Dead lift (Figs. 3.4 and 3.5)

Starting position. Body in squat position, that is, thighs are approximately parallel to floor, and feet are 8"–12" apart. Hands are shoulder width apart, grip alternating or pronated; arms are straight. Head is up, and back is at a 25–30 degree angle, flat, and arched at the base.

Movement. Taking a deep breath, keeping the arms straight, the back in a locked position, stand erect by driving upward as long as possible with the power generated by the hips and legs. It should not be necessary to use the back fully until the bar passes the knees. Do not "jerk" the weight

Fig. 3.4 Starting position for the dead lift and the power lift.

Fig. 3.5 Dead lift

off the floor by straightening the legs, bending the arms, and rounding the back. Serious injury can result from not maintaining the back in a fixed and locked position at the start of the lift. At the completion of a heavy lift, "ease" the weight back to the original starting position by sliding the bar down the thighs. When executing more than one repetition, avoid bouncing the bar off the floor.

Major muscles exercised

1. Quadriceps—P.M.
2. Glutaeus maximus, hamstrings—P.M.
3. Erector spinae—Asst.
4. Abdominal and hip flexors—Asst.

2. Power clean (Figs. 3.6 and 3.7)

Starting position. Assume same starting position as outlined for dead lift except position the shoulders forward of bar.

Movement. The initial pull, supplied by the legs and hips, is strong and slow. As the bar passes 4 to 5 inches above the kneecaps, accelerate the pull by extending on the toes and driving the hips upward and forward. Throughout this "second" pull, raise the elbows high and out to the sides and keep the bar close to the body. At the top of the pull, with the bar approximately chest high, duck quickly under the bar by bending the legs and whipping the elbows under to catch the weight. When power cleaning heavy weights, move the feet slightly out to the sides at the top of the pull (this movement permits the lifter to obtain a lower position. Once the bar is fixed on the chest, stand erect for completion of the lift.

Remember, on the initial pull *do not* jerk the bar off the floor by bending the arms and straightening the legs. Always keep the back flat and arched at the base.

Fig. 3.6 Power clean

Fig. 3.7 In power cleaning, the technique for lifting maximum weights is the same as for lighter ones.

Major muscles exercised

1. Quadriceps—P.M.
2. Glutaeus maximus, hamstrings—P.M.
3. Erector spinae—Asst.
4. Abdominal and hip flexors—Asst.
5. Deltoids—P.M.
6. Trapezius, upper—Asst.
7. Biceps—Asst.
8. Radial flexors—Asst.

2a. "Dead hang" power clean

Starting position. In executing repetitions in the power clean with light and medium loads, the bar is lowered to a point below the knees but still several inches from the floor. From this dead hung position, the bar is again cleaned to the chest.

Movement. Following the initial clean to the chest, lower the bar to an upright hang position so that you are standing erect with the bar at arm's length across the thighs. From this position bend forward at the hips and assume the starting dead hung position which is the same as for the regular clean except the weight is not touching the floor. Do not hold this hang position but in one continuous movement clean the bar to the chest. Practicing this movement will improve technique and develop a strong second pull.

3. Military press, standing (Figs. 3.8 and 3.9)

Starting position. Same starting position as for power clean, with shoulder width pronated grip. Military press may also be performed in a seated position (Fig. 3.10).

Fig. 3.8 Standing military press, starting position

Fig. 3.9 Standing military press   **Fig. 3.10** Seated military press

Movement.   Clean the bar to the chest, pause and assume the "get set" position: feet parallel, 12–14 inches apart; knees locked; head up; eyes focused slightly upward and ahead; elbows in at the sides; bar resting across the upper chest and shoulders. Take a deep breath and simultaneously contract the hips, thighs, and abdominal muscles, vigorously pressing the bar overhead by using arm and shoulder power. Throughout the movement keep the knees in a locked position, feet flat, and permit no excessive bending of the back.

Major muscles exercised (Fig. 3.11)

1.   Deltoids—P.M.
2.   Upper pectoralis major—Asst.
3.   Latissimus dorsi—Asst. (stabilizer)
4.   Triceps—P.M.

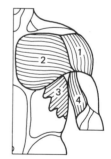

Fig. 3.11 Major muscles exercised in military press

4. Press behind neck (Fig. 3.12)

Starting position.   Using pronated grip, slightly wider than shoulder width, clean to the chest and press overhead.

Movement.   From the overhead position, lower the bar to behind the head, touching the base of the neck; then press to the overhead position.

Major muscles exercised

1.   Deltoids (middle and anterior)—P.M.
2.   Triceps—P.M.
3.   Upper trapezius—Asst.

Fig. 3.12 Press behind neck

5. Bench press (Fig. 3.13)

Starting position. Supine position on bench with head on bench. Using pronated grip slightly wider than shoulder width, hold bar at arm's length above chest.

Movement. Inhale, then lower bar to the chest, touching lightly; with a vigorous arm, shoulder, and chest drive (no bounce or heave permitted), press to the starting position and exhale. When bench pressing maximum or near maximum loads, lower the bar slowly so as to permit complete control of the weight at all times. Throughout the pressing movement, the buttocks must remain in contact with the bench, with the elbows

Fig. 3.13 Bench press

positioned either in at the sides or pointed outwards; practice will determine the most comfortable position.

6. Incline press (Fig. 3.14)

Starting position. Clean bar to chest and then carefully step back to incline bench.

Movement. Use the same technique as in the bench press, except that at the start of the incline press the bar will be on the chest. The initial press gets you to the extended-arms position, which, as in the bench press, is the starting point. Remember that inhalation takes place when you are in the starting position.

Major muscles exercised (bench press and incline press)

1. Anterior deltoids—P.M.
2. Upper and middle pectoralis major—P.M.
3. Latissimus major—Asst.
4. Triceps—P.M.

Fig. 3.14 Incline press

7. Dumbbell press (Fig. 3.15)

Dumbbell pressing may be performed from a standing, seated, inclined, or supine position. You may press the dumbbells simultaneously or alternately. Be sure to hold the palms of the hands forward when pressing.

Major muscles exercised

1. Deltoids (middle and anterior)—P.M.
2. Triceps—P.M.
3. Pectoralis major—Asst.
4. Upper trapezius—Asst.

Fig. 3.15 Dumbbell press, seated

8. Upright row (Fig. 3.16)

Starting position. Pronated grip, hands almost touching, arms extended.

Movement. Lift the bar up to the chin, keeping the elbows high and keeping the bar near the body. On the downward movement, do not let the bar drop without resistance.

Major muscles exercised

1. Trapezius—P.M.
2. Middle deltoids—P.M.
3. Biceps—Asst.
4. Brachioradialis—Asst.
5. Brachialis—Asst.

Fig. 3.16 Upright row

Fig. 3.17 Bent-over row

9. Bent-over row (Fig. 3.17)

Starting position. Pronated grip, hands wider than shoulder width apart, upper trunk parallel to floor.

Movement. Keeping the back almost parallel to the floor and the knees locked, bring the bar up to the chest or stomach and return to the starting position. Again, do not let the bar drop without resistance on the downward movement.

Major muscles exercised

1. Trapezius—P.M.
2. Latissimus dorsi—P.M.
3. Posterior deltoids—P.M.
4. Radial flexor—Asst.

10. Two-hands curl (Figs. 3.18, 3.19, and 3.20)

Starting position.   Use supinated grip, elbows in at sides, and arms extended. This may be done from either a standing or inclined position, or standing with the arms extended to an inclined board.

Fig. 3.18 Two-hands curl

Fig. 3.19 Two-hands curl

Fig. 3.20 Two-hands curl

Movement.   Curl the bar up to the shoulders and then return to the starting position. Check to avoid unnecessary body movement and letting the bar drop without resistance.

10a. Dumbbell curl (Fig. 3.21)

Dumbbell curls may be performed simultaneously or alternately from a standing, seated, or inclined position; the last is the most effective position for biceps development. Keep the palms of the hands forward during the execution of the exercise.

Major muscles exercised (two-hands curl and dumbbell curl)

1. Biceps—P.M.
2. Radial flexors—Asst.
3. Brachioradialis—P.M.

Fig. 3.21 Dumbbell curl   **Fig. 3.22** Reverse curl

11. Reverse curl (Fig. 3.22)

Starting position. Use pronated grip, elbows in at sides, and arms extended.

Movement. Curl the bar up to the chest and then return to the starting position, keeping the elbows in at the sides at all times.

Major muscles exercised

1. Biceps—P.M.
2. Brachialis—P.M.
3. Brachioradialis—P.M.
4. Long radial extensor of wrists—Asst.

12. Pulldown, using latissimus (lat) machine (Fig. 3.23)

Starting position. Use wide pronated grip; perform the exercise in seated or kneeling position.

Movement. Pull the bar down until it touches the base of the neck. To avoid using the body as a counterweight, be sure to maintain contact with the bench.

Major muscles exercised

1. Latissimus dorsi—P.M.
2. Middle and lower trapezius—Asst.
3. Upper pectoralis major—Asst.
4. Brachioradialis—Asst.

Fig. 3.23 Pulldown   **Fig. 3.24** Triceps extension, using lat machine

13. Triceps extension, using lat machine (Fig. 3.24)

Starting position. Use pronated grip, hands close together, elbows in, and bar at eye level.

Movement. Press downward to full extension of the elbows, using the triceps as prime mover, and return slowly to starting position. Throughout the exercise avoid unnecessary body movement.

Major muscles exercised

1. Triceps—P.M.
2. Latissimus dorsi—Asst.
3. Radial flexors—P.M.
4. Brachioradialis—Asst.

14. Triceps extension, supine (Fig. 3.25)

Starting position. Lying on bench, use pronated grip, slightly narrower than shoulder width, elbows in, with bar resting on bench behind the head.

Fig. 3.25 Triceps extension, supine

Movement.   Raise the bar to a position directly over the chest, arms fully extended, then return slowly to the starting position. Keep the elbows in as close to the head as possible throughout the exercise.

Major muscles exercised

1.   Triceps—P.M.
2.   Anterior deltoids—Asst.

15. Shoulder shrug (Fig. 3.26)

Starting position.   Pronated or alternating grip, with arms extended.

Movement.   Shrug the shoulders vigorously up and back, breathing deeply.

Major muscles exercised

1.   Trapezius (upper)—P.M.
2.   Latissimus dorsi—Asst.

Fig. 3.26 Shoulder shrug

16. Parallel bar dip (Fig. 3.27)

Starting position. Arms supporting the body in suspended position between the parallel bars.

Movement. Dip downward as far as possible and return to the starting position. Avoid unnecessary body swing. You can add resistance by using a belt with a short chain weight.

Major muscles exercised

1. Deltoids—P.M.
2. Triceps—P.M.
3. Pectoralis major, sternal—P.M.
4. Latissimus dorsi—Asst. (stabilizer)
5. Radial flexors—Asst.

Fig. 3.27 Parallel bar dip

17. Lateral raise, dumbbells (Fig. 3.28)

Starting position. Hold dumbbells, touching, in front of body; arms are extended, grip pronated.

Movement. Raise both arms out to the sides of the body and on to an overhead position. Return to starting position by the same path of movement. Throughout the exercise, keep the arms as straight as possible and avoid unnecessary body swing.

Fig. 3.28 Lateral raise, dumbbells

Major muscles exercised

1. Deltoids (middle and anterior)—P.M.
2. Trapezius, serratus anterior, rhomboids—Asst.

18. Forward raise, dumbbells (Fig. 3.29)

Starting position. Pronated grip with arms hanging at sides.

Movement. Alternately raise the arms directly out to the front of the body and on upward to an overhead position and then return to starting position.

Major muscles exercised

1. Deltoids (anterior and middle)—P.M.
2. Pectoralis major (upper)—P.M.
3. Serratus anterior—Asst.
4. Trapezius—Asst.

Fig. 3.29 Forward raise, dumbbells

19. Supine lateral raise, dumbbells (Fig. 3.30)

Starting position. Supine position with dumbbells at arm's length above chest, palms facing in.

Movement. Take a deep breath and lower the dumbbells outward to the sides, then return to starting position. When using heavy dumbbells, keep the elbows slightly bent, as in the illustration, to reduce strain on the shoulders and elbows.

Major muscles exercised

1. Anterior deltoids—P.M.
2. Pectoralis major—P.M.
3. Serratus anterior—Asst.

Fig. 3.30 Supine lateral raise, dumbbells

20. Pullover, with bent arms (Fig. 3.31)

Starting position. Supine position with head hanging over the end of bench. Pronated grip.

Movement. Keeping the elbows flexed and close to the head, pull the weight from the floor over to the chest and return to starting position.

Major muscles exercised

1. Posterior deltoids—P.M.
2. Lower pectoralis major—P.M.
3. Latissimus dorsi—Asst.
4. Serratus anterior—Asst.

Fig. 3.31 Pullover, with bent arms

Fig. 3.32 Standing dumbbell swing

LOWER-BACK EXERCISES

21. Standing dumbbell swing (Fig. 3.32)

Starting position. One dumbbell held overhead and gripped with both hands. Knees slightly flexed, feet shoulder width apart.

Movement. Swing the dumbbell down between the legs and return to starting position, keeping the arms straight throughout the movement.

Major muscles exercised

1. Quadriceps—P.M.
2. Glutaeus maximus, hamstrings—P.M.
3. Erector spinae—P.M.
4. Abdominals—Asst.

22. Good morning exercise (Fig. 3.33)

Starting position.   Feet shoulder width apart, knees locked, and bar resting across shoulders.

Movement.   Bend forward from the hips until the trunk is parallel with the floor and return to starting position. When using a heavy weight, bend the knees slightly.

Major muscles exercised
1.   Quadriceps—P.M.
2.   Glutaeus maximus, hamstrings—P.M.
3.   Erector spinae—P.M.
4.   Abdominals—Asst.

Fig. 3.33 Good morning exercise

Fig. 3.34 Stiff-legged dead lift

23. Stiff-legged dead lift (Fig. 3.34)

Starting position.   Standing position, with bar held in front of body, arms straight, grip pronated. May be performed on a bench.

Movement.   Bend forward from the hips until the trunk is parallel with the floor. Return to the starting position. Keep the knees in a locked position throughout the movement.

Major muscles exercised
1.   Erector spinae—P.M.
2.   Glutaeus maximus, hamstrings—P.M.
3.   Abdominals—Asst.
4.   Trapezius—Asst.

24. Back hyperextension (Fig. 3.35)

Starting position.   Prone position, upper trunk unsupported over edge of table, partner sitting on legs. Hands are locked together behind head or holding a weight behind head.

Movement.   Bend downward from the waist until head points toward floor. Return to the starting position arching the back as high as possible. Try holding this arched position for a 2- or 3-second count.

Major muscles exercised

1.   Erector spinae—P.M.
2.   Glutaeus maximus, hamstrings—P.M.
3.   Abdominals—Asst.

Fig. 3.35 Back hyperextension   **Fig. 3.36** Squat (deep-knee bend)

25. Squat (deep-knee bend) (Fig. 3.36)

Starting position.   Bar resting across shoulders, head up, back flat, small of back arched, feet spaced 12–14 inches apart.

Movement.   Inhale deeply and squat slowly to a position at which the tops of the thighs are parallel to the floor. From this squat position drive upward, remembering to *keep the lower back arched* and fixed throughout the movement. Rounding the back places great stress on the vertebrae, which can result in serious injury. The squat is an excellent exercise for strengthening the ligaments of the knees, but avoid placing unnecessary strain on them by "bouncing" out of a low squat position. As an added safety measure, you may use a bench allowing you to squat parallel. If you find difficulty in maintaining balance, you should try the exercise with a block placed under your heels.

Major muscles exercised

1.   Quadriceps—P.M.
2.   Glutaeus maximus, hamstrings—P.M.
3.   Erector spinae—P.M.

25a. Front squat (Fig. 3.37)

The same technique is used as in the regular squat except that the bar is held on the chest.

25b. Hack squat (Fig. 3.38)

The technique is the same as for a regular squat except that the bar is held behind the legs and the heels are elevated on a block. This exercise may also be performed on a "Hack machine."

Fig. 3.37 Front squat

Fig. 3.38 Hack squat

26. Leg extension (Fig. 3.39)

Starting position. This exercise may be performed with an iron boot or a leg extension machine. Seated position, knees flexed.

Movement. Extend the legs fully and hold in this position for a 2- or 3-second count, then return slowly to the starting position. Leg extensions and back squats are highly recommended for prevention and treatment of knee injuries.

Major muscles exercised
1. Quadriceps—P.M.

Fig. 3.39 Leg extension

27. Leg curl (Fig. 3.40)

Starting position.   This exercise may be performed with an iron boot or a leg extension machine. Prone position, legs extended.

Movement.   Flex at the knee joint until the foot is over the buttocks and return slowly to the starting position.

Major muscles exercised

1.   Hamstrings—P.M.
2.   Glutaeus maximus—Asst.

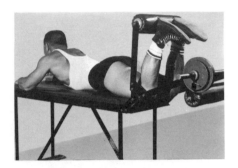

Fig. 3.40 Leg curl   **Fig. 3.41** Toe raise

28. Toe raise (Fig. 3.41)

Starting position.   This exercise may be performed using either a "calf machine" or a bar across the shoulders. Feet should be 6–8 inches apart.

Movement.   Rise up on the toes, concentrating on full extension. Hold this position for a 2-second count. The calves respond slowly to exercise and therefore require much hard work. Repetitions of 15 to 20 are recommended.

Major muscles exercised

1.   Gastrocnemius—P.M.
2.   Soleus—P.M.

ABDOMINAL EXERCISES

29. Sit-up (Fig. 3.42)

Starting position.   Hook-lying position, legs bent at knees, hands behind head supporting a weight. Whether in long-lying or hook-lying position, activity of the hip flexors is increased when the feet are held down, and activity of the abdominals is increased when they are not held down.

Fig. 3.42 Sit-up

Movement Sit up, touching elbows to knees. Curl back down to starting position. A trunk twist may be added by touching one elbow to the opposite knee. Adding resistance to such a twist brings all of the trunk rotators into action.

Major muscles exercised

1. Abdominals—P.M.
2. Obliques, external and internal—P.M.
3. Sternocleidomastoid—Asst.

30. Double leg raise (Fig. 3.43)

Starting position. Hanging position, feet free from ground.

Movement. Flex at the hip joint, keeping the knees locked until the legs are parallel to the ground. Raising the legs straight requires contraction of the abdominals against strong resistance, with the contraction tending to be static. Hip flexion predominates over spine flexion.

Major muscles exercised

1. Abdominals—P.M.

Fig. 3.43 Double leg raise

NECK EXERCISES (using head harness and weights)

31. Neck flexor (Fig. 3.44)

Starting position.   Sitting or supine position on bench.

Movement.   Curl or flex the head forward until chin touches or approaches the chest. Lower or extend the head slowly back to the maximal stretch position.

Major muscles exercised
1.   Sternocleidomastoid—P.M.
2.   Prevertebral muscles—Asst.

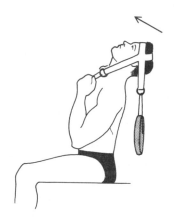

Fig. 3.44 Neck flexor

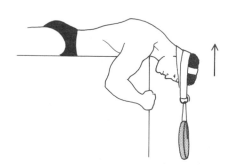

Fig. 3.45 Neck extensor

32. Neck extensor (Fig. 3.45)

Starting position.   Prone position, chest and shoulders resting on table. Legs are straight and arms are at sides for support.

Movement.   Extend the head up and backward as far as possible in an attempt to touch the back of the head to the cervical spine.

Major muscles exercised
1.   Deep posterior muscles, cervical region—P.M.
2.   Trapezius (upper)—Asst.

A summary of the exercises described in the preceding pages, with muscles affected by each, is given in the appendix to this chapter. Also included are front and back muscle charts which show the locations of the muscles involved (Figs. 3.46 and 3.47).

REFERENCE

1. Grimek, J. C., "How Much Should You Measure." *Muscular Development* **1**, No. 1: 17–19 (1964).

SUPPLEMENTARY READING

Rasch, P. J., and R. K. Burke, *Kinesology and Applied Anatomy*. Philadelphia: Lea and Febiger, 1959.

APPENDIX

TABLE 3.2 Muscles Affected by Various Exercises

Exercise	Number	Body Area	Body Surface	Muscles
Dead lift	1	Trunk	Posterior Anterior	Quadriceps, Glutaeus Maximus, Hamstrings, Erector spinae
Power clean	2	Trunk Shoulder Girdle	Posterior Anterior	Quadriceps, Glutaeus maximus, Hamstrings, Erector spinae, Abdominal and hip flexors, Deltoid, Trapezius, Biceps, Radial flexor
Standing military press	3	Shoulder Upper Arm	Anterior Superior Posterior	Deltoids, Upper pectoralis major, Latissimus dorsi, Triceps
Press behind neck	4	Shoulder	Superior Anterior Posterior	Deltoids (middle and anterior), Triceps, Upper trapezius

(cont.)

TABLE 3.2 (continued)

Exercise	Number	Body Area	Body Surface	Muscles
Bench press Incline press	5–6	Chest Upper Arm	Anterior Posterior	Anterior deltoids, Upper and middle pectoralis major, Latissimus dorsi
Dumbbell press	7	Shoulder	Superior Anterior Posterior	Deltoids (middle and anterior), Triceps, Pectoralis major, Upper trapezius
Upright row	8	Shoulder	Superior	Trapezius, Middle deltoids, Biceps, Brachioradialis, Brachialis
Bent-over row	9	Shoulder Girdle	Posterior	Trapezius, Latissimus dorsi, Rhomboides, Posterior deltoids, Radial flexors
Two-hands curl	10	Upper Arm Lower Arm	Anterior	Biceps, Radial flexors, Brachioradialis
Reverse curl	11	Lower Arm	Anterior Posterior	Biceps, Brachialis, Brachioradialis, Long radial extensors of wrists
Pulldown, lat machine	12	Shoulder Girdle	Anterior Posterior	Latissimus dorsi, Trapezius, Upper pectoralis major
Triceps extension, lat machine	13	Upper & Lower Arm	Anterior Posterior	Triceps, Latissimus dorsi, Flexor radialis, Brachioradialis
Triceps extension, supine	14	Shoulder Upper Arm	Anterior Posterior	Anterior deltoids, Triceps
Shoulder shrug	15	Shoulder	Superior	Trapezius, Latissimus dorsi
Parallel bar dip	16	Shoulder Upper & Lower Arm	Anterior Superior Posterior	Deltoids, Triceps, Pectoralis major, Latissimus dorsi
Lateral raise, dumbbells	17	Shoulder	Superior	Deltoids, Trapezius, Serratus anterior
Forward raise, dumbbells	18	Shoulder	Anterior	Deltoids (anterior and middle), Pectoralis major, Serratus anterior, Trapezius
Supine lateral raise, dumbbells	19	Shoulder Chest	Anterior	Anterior deltoids, Pectoralis major, Serratus anterior

TABLE 3.2 (continued)

Exercise	Number	Body Area	Body Surface	Muscles
Pullovers, bent arms	20	Chest	Anterior Posterior	Posterior deltoids, Lower pectoralis major, Latissimus dorsi, Serratus anterior
Standing dumbbell swing	21	Lower Back	Posterior	Quadriceps, Glutaeus maximus, Hamstrings, Erector spinae, Abdominals
Good morning exercise	22	Lower Back	Posterior Anterior	Quadriceps, Glutaeus maximus, Hamstrings, Erector spinae, Abdominals
Stiff-legged dead lift	23	Lower Back	Posterior	Trapezius, Erector spinae, Glutaeus maximus, Hamstrings, Abdominals
Back hypertension	24	Lower Back	Posterior	Erector spinae, Glutaeus maximus, Hamstrings, Abdominals
Squat	25	Lower & Upper Back Upper Legs	Posterior Anterior	Glutaeus maximus, Quadriceps, Abdominals, Erector spinae
Leg extension	26	Upper Leg	Anterior	Quadriceps Vastus lateralis Vastus medialis Rectus femoris
Leg curl	27	Upper Legs	Posterior Anterior	Hamstrings, Gluteus maximus
Toe raise	28	Lower Leg	Posterior	Gastrocnemius, Soleus
Sit-ups	29	Trunk	Anterior	Sternocleidomastoids, Abdominals, Obliques
Double-leg raise	30	Trunk	Anterior	Abdominals
Neck flexor	31	Neck	Anterior	Prevertebral muscles, Sternocleidomastoids
Neck extensor	32	Neck	Posterior	Deep posterior muscles cervical region, Trapezius (upper)

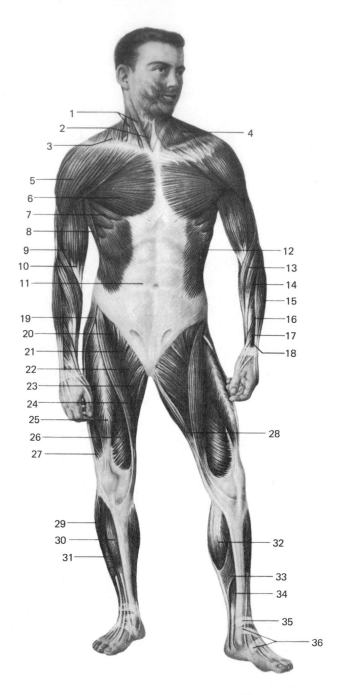

Fig. 3.46 Muscles and muscle groups (front). (Courtesy of Merck Sharp & Dohme)

1. Sternocleidomastoid (M. sternocleidomastoideus)
2. Sternohyoid (M. sternohyoideus)
3. Trapezius
4. Flat (M. platysma)
5. Deltoid (M. deltoideus)
6. Pectoralis major
7. Serratus anterior
8. Latissimus dorsi
9. Brachial (brachialis)
10. Biceps (M. biceps brachii)
11. Rectus abdominis
12. External oblique (M. obliquus abdominis externus)
13. Brachioradialis
14. Long radial extensor of wrist (M. extensor carpi radialis longus)
15. Common extensor of fingers (M. extensor digitorum communis)
16. Short radial extensor of wrist (M. extensor carpi radialis brevis)
17. Long abductor of thumb (M. abductor pollicis longus)
18. Short extensor of thumb (M. extensor pollicis brevis)
19. Tensor of broad fasciae (M. tensor fasciae latae)
20. Iliac (M. iliacus)

Hip flexor group

21. Psoas major
22. Pectineus
23. Long adductor
24. Sartorius
25. Rectus femoris

Quadriceps

25. Rectus femoris
26. Vastus medialis
27. Vastus lateralis
28. Slender (M. gracilis)
29. Peronaeus longus
30. Anterior tibial
31. Long extensor of toes (M. extensor digitorum longus)
32. Gastrocnemius
33. Soleus
34. Long flexor of toe (M. flexor digitorum longus)
35. Transverse ligament (Lig. transversum cruris)
36. Cruciate ligament (Lig. cruciatum cruris)

Key for Fig. 3.46

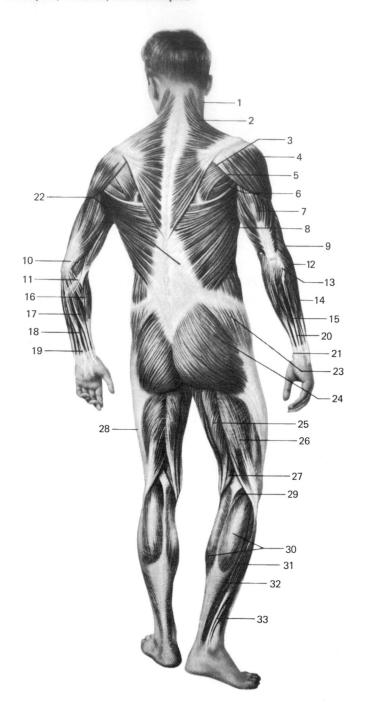

Fig. 3.47 Muscles and muscle groups (back). (Courtesy of Merck Sharp & Dohme)

1. Sternocleidomastoid
2. Trapezius
3. Infraspinous
4. Deltoid
5. Teres minor
6. Teres major
7. Triceps
8. Latissimus dorsi
9. Brachioradialis
10. Brachialis
11. Pronator teres
12. Long radial extensor of wrist (M. extensor carpi radialis longus)
13. Anconeus
14. Common extensor of fingers (M. extensor digitorum communis)
15. Ulnaris extensor of wrist (M. extensor carpi ulnaris)
16. Brachioradialis
17. Radial flexor (M. flexor carpi radialis)
18. Superficial flexor of fingers (M. flexor digitorum sublimis)
19. Palmaris longus
20. Extensor of flfth finger
21. Ulna flexor
22. Erector spinae
23. Middle gluteal (M. glutaeus medius)
24. Glutaeus maximus

Hamstring Group
25. Semitendinous
26. Biceps femoris
27. Semimembranosus
28. Tensor of broad fascial
29. Plantaris
30. Gastrocnemius
31. Peronaeus longus
32. Soleus
33. Short Peroneal (M. peronaeus brevis)

Key for Fig. 3.47

4

aerobic
weight training

A general belief held by weightlifters is that cardiovascular fitness is obtained through weight training. As discussed in Chapter 1, conventional forms of weight training fall into the "aerobic" exercise category. Thus, weightlifting has very little training effect on the heart, lungs, and circulatory system. More specifically, weightlifting increases the force of skeletal muscle contraction which in turn increases strength and body power. The very nature of the exercise—medium to heavy resistance with short burst of exertion, followed by several minutes of rest—is not conducive to cardiovascular development. This training characteristic is especially true of Olympic lifting where strength is the primary goal and physical exertion lasts only a few seconds at the most. In weightlifting, then, the energy for muscle contraction is obtained through the anaerobic chemical process.

As a result of intensive research in exercise physiology, Cooper [1] has laid down two basic principles regarding aerobic training and the development of cardiovascular fitness.

1. If the exercise is vigorous enough to produce a sustained heart rate of 150 beats per minute or more, the training-effect benefits begin about five minutes after the exercise starts and continue as long as the exercise is performed.
2. If the exercise is not vigorous enough to produce a sustained heart rate of 150 beats per minute, even though it demands extra oxygen, the exercise must be continued considerably longer than five minutes, the total period of time depending on the oxygen consumed.

With these principles in mind, we can see why weightlifting is not a suitable form of training for developing or maintaining cardiovascular-respiratory fitness.

AEROBIC WEIGHT TRAINING

One method of weightlifting that will tax the cardiovascular-respiratory system and bring about a significant improvement in its function is "aerobic weight training," the application of the "interval" training concept to conventional weightlifting exercises. The interval training concept is based upon 1–2 minutes of maximum exercise with a recovery period of 30–90 seconds. A rest interval of longer than 90 seconds is not interval training. During interval training the heart rate must reach a maximum of 180 beats and return to 120 during the rest interval. This applies only to athletes between the ages of 18 and 30 (see Table 9.7). If the heart rate does not recover to 120–130 beats in 90 seconds, the interval has been too long or too hard. This system of aerobic weight training causes the heart, lungs, and circulatory system to work far beyond demands placed on them by conventional weight training methods. As a result of taking a twelve-week course in aerobic weight training, students at Oregon State University recorded a significant improvement in aerobic power as measured by Astrand's Estimated Oxygen Up-take Capacity Test [2].

Aerobio weight training permits a balance between aerobic and anaerobic processes to be maintained in a steady state at a high level of work, with a constant concentration of lactic acid in the blood. Tolerance for both aerobic and anaerobic work can gradually be increased in duration and Intensity so that the traInee adapts himself to endure a high level of discomfort. The results of aerobic weight training are: (1) cardiac output is greatly increased, (2) respiratory efficiency is improved, and (3) the muscle fatigue factor in training is reduced.

Aerobic weight training serves as an excellent conditioner for all types of sports and activities that demand a high level of total fitness. Its use as a pre-season conditioner has been recommended by prominent coaches [3] who demand total fitness of their athletes. For pre-season conditioning, aerobic weight training sessions are scheduled three times a week on alternate days from the regular heavy-strength program undertaken twice a week. During the competitive season, aerobic circuit training should be continued on a twice-a-week schedule with the primary objective being to maintain, not improve, the high level of cardiovascular and muscular endurance developed during the off-season and pre-season training programs.

Techniques of circuit weight training

Circuit weight training requires the trainee to exercise in short, all-out bursts of 45 seconds' duration, then rest for periods of one minute or less. The total number of repetitions executed during the 45 seconds of exercise should be set at a minimum of 15 and a maximum of 20. Once the trainee reaches this upper limit, he should increase the load. A circuit of eight or more stations is established with a specific exercise executed at each station. Exercises are selected so that none of the major muscle groups of the body are neglected. Exercises are also arranged in the circuit so that there is an alternation of arm, leg, shoulder, and back movements. Arrangement of this order will prevent fatiguing any one muscle group before the circuit has been completed. Using an eight-station circuit as an example, the following selection of exercises is recommended.

Circuit A	Circuit B
Bench Press	Incline Press
Squat	Hack Squat
Pullover (bent or straight arm)	Leg Raise
Upright Row	Curl, in seated position with dumbbells
Dead Lift	Parallel Bar Dip
Lat-machine, behind the neck	Standing Lateral Raise
Sit-up	Bent-over Row
Curl	Power Snatch

Note: The military press is omitted because it places a great amount of stress on the muscles of the lower back.

Organizational procedures

The organization of a group (class or team) for aerobic circuit training will depend on the number of trainees, size of the training facility, and the amount of available equipment. Usually, less equipment is required for circuit training than for regular weightlifting, since the training weight loads are far below maximum. Assuming that the group contains 32 trainees or athletes, there should be two sections, each having its own circuit of eight stations. When the group is split, the stronger individuals should be in one half so that heavier training loads can be utilized in their circuit, thus the weaker trainees can use appropriate weights for their group as well. With two trainees as partners, one exercises while the other serves as spotter and coach, keeping count of the repetitions performed. The instructor keeps time and gives the commands to start and stop exercising and to change stations.

Aerobic weight training is strenuous cardiovascular and muscular work, and it generally requires several training periods before all trainees adjust themselves to it. At first the less fit may require a longer rest between stations, and a few may experience nausea as a symptom of going "all out." However, as the training progresses, all will adjust and learn to push themselves as nearly as possible to the limits of their muscular endurance. One of the objectives of aerobic circuit training is to show the trainee that the point of psychological exhaustion can be pushed back, permitting the entire body to be brought close to actual physical exhaustion.

When the group have conditioned themselves mentally and physically to aerobic circuit training, the severity of the workouts should be gradually increased. This is accomplished by: (1) increasing the number of training stations, (2) repeating the circuit, (3) increasing the weight loads, (4) reducing the rest interval, and (5) increasing the exercise time.

Measuring Changes in Cardiovascular Function

Because of its close relationship to cardiac output and oxygen consumption, the heart rate is a good indicator of the stress imposed by muscular activity on the heart. The pulse rate, as a single factor, quite accurately depicts the cardiovascular adjustment of an individual to muscular exercise. To determine the effects of aerobic weight training on the heart, the "start pulse" (pre-exercise heart rate) is taken in a standing position for a 15-second count (start pulse $\times$ 15 seconds = 1-minute heart rate) before exercising. Immediately following the completion of the training, the heart rate is taken again (postexercise heart rate) at one minute intervals until it returns to approximately 100 beats. In the fit individual this should take no longer than two to three minutes. Overall, the postexercise heart rate will return close (3–5 beats) to the pre-exercise rate in 30 to 35 minutes. The ability of the heart to recover more quickly to the pre-exercise rate is considered an excellent indicator of one's adjustment to aerobic work.

A more accurate assessment of an individual's aerobic work capacity can be obtained through the 1.5-mile cardiovascular fitness run (see Chapter 9). This test requires long-lasting exertion, thus it taxes the heart and lungs long enough to permit these systems to establish and maintain a relatively high steady state. By relatively, we mean that sufficient oxygen is being delivered to the working muscles and also that the muscles are able to utilize this oxygen at a rate which will permit the individual to run the test distance in good or better time.

Measuring muscular endurance

The effects of aerobic circuit training on the development of muscular endurance can be determined by:

a) the time required to complete a circuit using a set percentage of body weight, performing each exercise for a predetermined number of repetitions (15–20). Trainees are started at one-minute intervals through the circuit and are scored on the time required to complete it. In using this method of testing, the instructor must equate body weight and the load to be used in testing. To serve as a guide, the following percentages are recommended for use in testing. The percentages may be modified in special situations where the loads prove to be too heavy, but in such cases, the individual is probably physically unfit for aerobic weight training and should be placed on a less severe strength-building routine.

Exercise	Percent of Body Weight Men	Women
Incline Press	50	20
Bench Press	60	40
Sit-up	10	5
Upright Row	30	20
Squat (to 14–16 inch bench)	90	60
Two Arm Curl	30	20
Parallel Bar Dips	body weight	–
Dead Lift	75	50

b) the improvement scored on the increase in the number of repetitions executed in a set time limit, using a set percentage of body weight. For example, using the three exercises and percentage of body weight listed below the student performs as many repetitions as possible in a two-minute period. During this two-minute test period the student may rest if necessary by having his partner relieve him of the weight for a few seconds. Again, the purpose of this test is to measure the endurance of specific muscle groups.

Exercise	Percent of Body Weight Men	Women
Bench Press	50	30
Squat (to 14–16 inch bench)	75	50
Sit-up	10	5

REFERENCES

1. Cooper, Kenneth H. *Aerobics.* New York: Evans & Co., 1968.

2. O'Shea, John P. "The effect of an eight-week aerobics weight team program on the development of cardiovascular endurance." Unpublished research data, Oregon State University, 1968.

3. Personal interviews by the author with Dr. Dale Thomas, wrestling coach, Oregon State University, and with Bill Winkler, swimming coach, Oregon State University.

functional
isometric training

Based upon the SAID principle, functional isometrics is an advanced training concept intended to push the athlete toward his ultimate physiological and psychological strength limits. The nature of this training requires the athlete to generate maximum dynamic strength in one explosive effort and then sustain this effort isometrically for a short duration; in other words, functional isometrics as a training concept combines isotonic and isometric muscle contractions into a unified movement. Today, this method of training is used extensively with great success by world-class strength athletes, such as shot-putters, hammer-throwers, and Olympic-style weightlifters.

Functional isometric training requires the use of a power rack with pins placed approximately 2 inches above the supports on which the barbell is resting. The loads used in this type of training are 90 percent or more of the lifter's 1-RM. After assuming a position the lifter drives the barbell with maximum body power up to the pins (isotonic phase), then holds it there (isometric phase) for a period of 3–5 seconds. Strong neuromuscular action is involved in overcoming the inertia of the barbell. Then, as the barbell is driven with force against the pins, the initial dynamic strength effort must be sustained in a strong static muscle contraction.

NEUROMUSCULAR INFLUENCE ON THE EXPRESSION OF STRENGTH

The cross-sectional area and the physiological state of a muscle will determine its ultimate functional capacity; however the actual performance fluctuates more rapidly and over a wider range than can be fully explained by changes in these factors. Therefore, the causes of rapid and reversible changes in muscle strength must be found in the neuromuscular system. Skeletal muscles are completely dependent upon the nervous system for their function in achieving muscle tension. Darcus [1] has stated that the changes that occur in the neuromuscular system due to training are of primary importance and that the muscular changes are secondary. Empirical evidence in support of Darcus can be seen in champion Olympic lifters who continue to improve their performance over a period of 5–8 years while maintaining a constant bodyweight. Their continuing strength gains may be attributed more to the influence of psychological factors upon the neuromuscular system than to purely physiological factors.

Although it is futile to attempt to make a clear distinction between the physiological and psychological factors, since both operate in the same nervous system, it is nevertheless helpful to attempt to separate them in our thinking. Physiological factors set the relatively fixed and outermost limits of strength; psychological factors the more proximate ones. In this context it is appropriate to speak of physiological and psychological limits of strength. The physiological limits of strength are fairly well understood, while the psychological limits are mostly unknown and difficult to measure.

In studying the effects of brief maximal exercise on the quadriceps femoris, Rose [2] concluded that "the persistence of strength as a learned act certainly does not appear to be an impossible concept." Based upon Rose's observation one may reason that the psychological factors—motivation, body image, and consciousness—are a crucial consideration in neuromuscular function and, ultimately, in the expression of human strength.

As one may see, the neuromuscular system plays a key role in functional isometric training. Through the application of the progressive overload principle to the techniques of functional isometric training, the strength athlete can gradually condition his neuromuscular system to express itself in terms of increased dynamic strength performance. The po-

Fig. 5.1 Jack "Mad Dog" O'Billovich, former Oregon State All-American, trains on functional isometrics.

tential value of functional isometrics, then, lies, in its ability to impose maximum stress on the psychological factors associated with high strength performance.

TECHNIQUES OF FUNCTIONAL ISOMETRICS

Best results are obtained by not resting too long between repetitions: about 2 minutes for maximum resistance, and $1/2$–1 minute for light or medium loads. Beginning with the upper body movements and then proceeding to the legs, a workout period should take approximately 45 minutes to an hour. For efficiency in training, a 3-partner group works best, providing just the proper rest interval and facilitating the changing and positioning of the weight.

When exercising with functional isometrics, the trainee must position himself carefully so that he is directly in the most effective line of pushing or pulling. For an exercise in which good leverage and large muscle groups come directly into play, the trainee should use as heavy a resistance as possible. For an exercise position where leverage is poor, there is a tendency for the trainee to cheat by allowing the larger muscle groups to do the work, rather than the specific muscle involved. This must be avoided if specific muscles are to be developed. For example, in executing the various pressing positions, the trainee should not use his legs to assist in the initial drive. Individual weaknesses are overcome only when the muscles directly involved in a specific movement are forced to do their work. Once in position to lift, the trainee musters all the explosive force within himself and drives the bar against the pins; then he sustains this powerful drive 3–5 seconds. He must take care to have the bar pressing only against the pins and not cornered between the pins and the upright supports of the power rack. There is a delicate balance involved in driving and holding the bar in position against the pin, and it requires several workouts before the neuro-muscular system can adapt itself.

Trial and error is the only method that can be used to determine the best starting poundage. One should not overload, but should give the body an opportunity to adapt itself to this type of training. Following the first few workouts, the trainee may experience sore wrist, shoulder, and knee joints. This is only a temporary situation and should disappear within a week of training. The trainee must guard against overwork for it will hinder progress rather than help.

FUNCTIONAL ISOMETRIC EXERCISES

In functional isometric training, there are approximately eight basic movements that can be performed: press, pull, squat, bench press, upright row, curl, bent-over row, and toe raise.

As practice for Olympic lifting events:

Four positions (pronated grip, see Figs. 5.2–5.5)

1. Jerk lockout (*not* a functional isometric)
2. Top of press (2–3 inches below lockout position)
3. Middle press (eye level)
4. Low press (drive starts 2 inches above chest)

Fig. 5.2 Jerk lockout

Fig 5.3 Top of press

Fig. 5.4 Middle press

Fig. 5.5 Low press

Pulls, three positions (pronated grip, using hand grips; see Figs. 5.6–5.8)

1. High pull (snatch grip, on toes, fully extended)
2. Middle pull (clean grip, middle of thigh)
3. Low pull (clean grip, 3–4 inches below knee)

Fig. 5.6 High pull

Fig. 5.7 Middle pull

Fig. 5.8 Low pull

Squats, three body positions (pronated grip, see Figs. 5.9–5.11)

1. High squat (just below knee lockout)
2. Middle squat (4 inches below position 1)
3. Low squat (4 inches below position 2)

Fig. 5.9 High squat ▶

Fig. 5.10 Middle squat

Fig. 5.11 Low squat ▶

For overall strength building:

1. Bench press (Fig. 5.12)   3 positions
2. Upright row (Fig. 5.13)   2 positions
3. Curl (Fig. 5.14)   2 positions
4. Bent-over row (Fig. 5.15)   2 positions
5. Squats   3 positions

Fig. 5.12 Bench press

Fig. 5.13 Upright row

◄ **Fig. 5.14** Curl

Fig. 5.15 Bent-over row ►

In scheduling functional isometric workouts in the training program, there are several arrangements that may be given consideration. For Olympic lifters, functional isometrics may be practiced three times a week as follows: Monday, medium, about 80 percent of maximum; Wednesday, maximum; Friday, about 80 percent of maximum; Saturday, maximum effort on only the Olympic lifts. On Tuesday and Thursday, the lifter should work to improve his skill and technique in the Olympic lifts with light form work and should run distances and sprints to improve cardiovascular fitness.

For strength athletes and Olympic lifters, training for two consecutive days and resting on the third has proved effective:

1st day—regular dynamic training

2nd day—functional isometrics

3rd day—rest

4th day—regular dynamic training

5th day—functional isometrics

6th day—rest

THE USE OF PURE ISOMETRIC OR STATIC CONTRACTION

In the past few years, pure isometric exercise has been widely acclaimed as a method by which athletes can build super strength. However, the nature of pure static exercise precludes (1) using the overload principle of training, (2) knowing how much muscle tension is exerted, (3) placing stress on the neuromuscular system, (4) measuring progress easily, and (5) causing the joints to work through any range of movement.

Pure isometrics may be useful when time or circumstances do not permit training with either dynamic movement or functional isometric movements. This type of training is beneficial in maintaining strength and muscle tone over a short period of time. Through personal experience, the author would estimate this period to be about three or four weeks. A portable isometric bar is convenient and compact to use on trips or vacations. All of the exercises recommended for functional isometrics can be performed on this portable bar. (See Figs. 5–16 through 5–20.)

Fig. 5.16 High press   **Fig. 5.17** Low squat   **Fig. 5.18** Two-hands curl

Fig. 5.19 Upright row   **Fig. 5.20** Low pull

REFERENCES

1. Darcus, H. D. "Discussion on an Evaluation of the Methods of Increased Muscle Strength." *Proceedings of the Royal Society of Medicine* **49**:999–1006 (December 1956).

2. Rose, D. L., et al. "Effects of Brief Maximal Exercise on the Quadriceps Femoris." *Archives of Physical Medicine and Rehabilitation* **38**:157–164 (March 1957).

6

strength training
for athletes

The second half of the twentieth century is emerging as the "Golden Age of Sport." Participation in both amateur and professional sports is at a level undreamed of only thirty years ago. World and national records are broken and rebroken with almost monotonous regularity. Winning times and distances in the 1968 Olympics in track and field and in swimming, impressive as they were, are now almost common accomplishments. Two decades ago, track authorities predicted the ultimate in the shot was 65 feet; the discus, 200 feet; the high jump, 7 feet; and the pole vault, 16 feet. Today these marks represent only the qualifying standards for national and international competition. In Olympic swimming competition, Johnny Weissmuller, the all-time great of the 1924 and 1928 Olympic Games, would be hard pressed to "place" in the women's 100-meter free style event. A similar situation exists in Olympic weightlifting, where featherweights exceed the totals posted by heavyweights in the 1936 Olympics. When John Davis, the world heavyweight champion, broke the 1000-lb barrier for the three Olympic lifts in 1947, who then would have predicted that today middleweights could do it and lightweights would be approaching it (providing the three lifts were still being used).

In this "jet age," there is no achievement that cannot be matched, no record that cannot be broken. There are a number of factors which account for this remarkable situation; a few of the most significant are given here:

1. Greater numbers of participants are competing in all sports, with competition now offered at all age levels.

2. Today is the era of the "specialist." Competition is so keen and intense that an athlete must channel all of his time and energy into one sport or event, and sports are no longer seasonal occupations. There is no super-athlete today who, upon completing a season of football or basketball, can turn out for track and field and put the shot 70 feet or pole vault 17 feet.

3. More and better coaching is available at all levels of competition. Young athletes no longer have to wait until they reach high school or college to receive good coaching; and their coaching is most often by specialists in the sport.

4. Psychological outlook has changed. Athletes no longer seem to be mentally inhibited by physiological limitations.

5. Technology has advanced in the design and construction of athletic equipment and facilities; for example, fiberglass vaulting poles have replaced aluminum poles, and tracks are now constructed of "all-weather material," making for ideal conditions for training and competition at all times.

6. The role of proper nutrition in improving athletic performances has received greater attention in the past ten years.

7. Finally, and quite possibly the most important factor in the current upsurge of record-breaking performances, athletes are adopting scientifically based weight training methods. For the majority of outstanding athletes today, weight training is an indispensable part of the off-season and pre-season program; and for many, it is an important part of the competitive season training as well.

Fig. 6.1 Gary Gubner, former National AAU Heavyweight weightlifting champion and former national collegiate shot put champion and indoor world record holder. (Courtesy of *Strength and Health*)

Quotations from Olympic stars emphasize the role weight training must play in every potential champion's training program [1].

Russ Hodge, National AAU Decathlon Champion: "Weight training is a must for all athletes. It has enabled me to gain sufficient strength to compensate for lack of skill in some events."

Al Oerter, three-time Olympic Champion, Discus: "I have trained with weights three times a week for several years now. I train for overall strength on the basic power exercises, using as much weight as possible at all times. I lift all year around, but during track season my weight workouts are shortened from two and one half hours to about two hours. Once a week I have a combined weight-training and throwing workout. I use the weights first and then throw. Some of my better throws have come on these combined workout days."

Fred Hansen, Olympic Champion Pole Vault: "I have used weight training to build strength for vaulting since my sophomore year in college. I train three times a week with the weights during the off-season and definitely recommend it for all vaulters."

Randy Matson, former World record holder, Shot Put: "A great deal of the recent improvement I have made has been due to lifting weights. I do a lot of bench presses and squats in particular."

One of the most frequently raised questions is how much strength is needed to compete successfully in skill and endurance types of activities. Prominent researchers in the field of sports medicine have written the following comments concerning the role of strength in athletes:

Davis and Logan [2]: "The development of endurance tends to depend upon a level of strength, in other words, strength is a primary prerequisite to endurance—increasing strength tends to increase endurance and a training program for the augmentation of endurance brings about some strength increase."

Morehouse [3]: "Strength of the working muscles is a limiting factor in endurance. A load easily carried by strong muscles may quickly exhaust weak ones."

McCloy [4]: "A prerequisite for the economical learning of a skill is possession of sufficient strength to perform a task."

Jesse [5] "Strength is basic to a maximum development of speed and stamina."

Morehouse and Rasch [6]: "It is not recognized that development of muscular strength is the primary factor in the increasing fight against joint injuries and vigorous physical condition is a prerequisite to safe participation in sports."

Logan [7]: "Strength is necessary for the stability of joints, particularly of the extremities; muscular endurance delays the onset of fatigue, allowing better reaction time and decreasing the susceptibility to injury." *

To be a top competitor, the athlete of the present generation must possess a high level of skill and athetic fitness. Adamson [8] defines athletic fitness as comprising muscular strength, muscular endurance, cardiovascular endurance, and muscular power. All these qualities are best developed through the stress and strain of the overload principle. Acquisition of fitness requires a vigorous training environment which must include progressive weight training.

Today, in the face of overwhelming scientific evidence, some coaches and athletes object, for various reasons, to weight training. They prefer instead to base their strength conditioning programs on heavy labor, calisthenics, gymnastics, running through the sand in combat boots, running through the surf, climbing stadium steps or mountains, or a few isometric drills, all of which have their limitations as means of developing

---

* For research concerning the effects of weight training on the development of strength, consult Chapter 2.

Fig. 6.2 Two of the greatest weight-trained shot-putters in collegiate history: Neil Steinhauer (left), whose record is 68′ 11″; and Lalcen Samsam, whose record is over 68′. They are fine examples of what sensible weight training can do for an athlete.

strength fitness. To a small degree they all develop strength; but, compared to weight training, each is limited by at least one of the following points:

1. Heavy manual labor is hard to find in our automated age.
2. Skill and strength are a prerequisite for participation in these programs.
3. Special equipment or terrain is necessary.
4. Muscles used in some particular sport are not developed.
5. It is not possible to apply the progressive overload principle.

The advantages of using weights for developing strength are overwhelming:

1. The progressive overload principle can be employed.
2. Weight programs can be designed to develop all or any specific muscles.

DESIGNING A PROGRAM FOR ATHLETES

As was stated earlier in this book, weight training is not a "dynamic wonder course." Depending on the athlete's inherited body type characteristics, it takes an average of two or three months before specific results are realized. However, when progressive weight training is properly applied, performances will improve and the time required to develop into a good varsity athlete or a potential record-breaking champion will be greatly reduced.

An effective heavy-resistance weight program must be based on sound physiological principles (Chapter 1), and these principles must be scientifically applied (Chapter 3). Too often in athletics, weight programs are based on educated guesswork and hearsay rather than on physiological principles. Hoffman, America's foremost Olympic weight lifting coach, was one of the first to develop a system of progressive weight training exercises for use by either competitive lifters or athletes. DeLorme [9], also, advocates a system of heavy resistive exercises for use in athletics, physical education, and physical medicine. From his investigations, DeLorme concluded that different types of training are needed to develop the desired quality (power, endurance, speed, and coordination) in any particular muscle. As a result of observation both on the athletic field and in clinical laboratories, DeLorme established the following principles:

1. Increase in dynamic strength can be accomplished by a few repetitions against strong resistance.

2. Increased performance of the cardiovascular system can be accomplished by many repetitions against slight resistance.

3. The two methods are not interchangeable; one cannot accomplish the results of the other.

Strength training objectives

The principal objectives of every athlete's weight program is the development of muscular strength, muscular power, and muscular endurance through the full range of movement of the various joints. Thus, the antagonistic and assistant muscles must be strengthened as well as the prime movers. Static or guided-apparatus work should serve only as a supplement to the regular dynamic weight program. Overuse of isometrics and guided-apparatus work hinders development of neuromuscular coordination and of the antagonistic and assistant muscles.

This point is illustrated in analyzing the full squat. In this exercise the athlete bends the knees till his thighs are below parallel, then stops, then straightens to the upright position. Squatting requires an active force of the muscles which displace the body downward, followed by a braking force of the antagonistic muscles which contract to stop the motion; the return to the standing position also involves an active effort and a braking effort. If the athlete performs this sequence of motions on a guided or static apparatus, he does not completely exercise all the body forces that would normally be involved, nor does he develop the skill and strength and coordination that woud otherwise be called upon.

The strength and power generated by the large muscle groups of the shoulders, lower trunk, and legs are a dominant factor in producing a good performance in most athletic endeavors requiring a high level of dynamic strength. The abdominal and thigh areas in particular are important. There is an old adage that an athlete will go only as far as his legs will carry him. However, many coaches and athletes have an aversion to heavy leg work, especially squats. They fear squats will result in overdevelopment of the thighs, slowing the athlete down, and possibly injuring the knees. There is no scientific foundation to their fears on either account. In fact, evidence (cited in Chapter 2) indicates that as the strength of a muscle increases so does speed. As for squats having a harmful effect on the knees, when the exercise is executed correctly, that is, by squatting down until the "tops," or fronts, of the thighs are parallel with the floor and then recovering, the chances of injury are extremely remote. The athlete should always lower into the squatting position slowly, so that he keeps the weight under control and is able to stop when the thighs reach the parallel position. Remember that dropping too rapidly into the squat position places an additional strain on the lower back and knees and leaves the way open to injuries.

Fig. 6.3 Full squats are an important part of Neil Steinhauer's workout.

Squats need to be a core exercise in every strength athlete's training program. Neil Steinhauer [10], former world indoor shot put record holder credited squats as a prime reason for his success. Some bystander might be inclined to say that Steinhauer was a "natural" and would have succeeded without the aid of squats. Well, there are *no* natural 70-foot shot-putters. An athlete such as Steinhauer has devoted years of hard and regular training to achieve what he did.

WEIGHT TRAINING CYCLES

Unless an athlete (male or female) is participating in more than one sport, he or she will achieve best results by training on a year-round basis. Training for strength, power, and endurance over a long period of time is more effective and lasting than short-term training. Concerning the retention of strength, Steinhaus [11] wrote that "rapid training induces only a loosely 'anchored' adjustment of the muscle to the measured demands made on it. If, however, this increased strength is maintained for a time it becomes fixated or anchored in the muscle." A year-round program is divided into three cycles—off-season, pre-season, and in-season. Individually, the cycles emphasize development of the fundamental qualities of fitness mentioned earlier.

Off-Season Cycle. Undoubtedly the most vital of the cycles is the off-season cycle, often referred to as the "power period," the cycle when total body strength and power are vastly increased. Lasting four to five months, the power program calls for maximum weight in both the core and specific exercises. Length and number of workouts should be set at a minimum of $1^1/2$ hours, four to five times a week. It is highly recommended that the progressive weight program be modeled after the one outlined in Chapter 3.

Functional isometrics, too, should play a role in this training cycle (see Chapter 5). This method of training is of special importance to such activities as shot-putting, hammer-throwing, discus, and javelin where strength is a prime factor in improving performance.

Pre-season Cycle. The pre-season cycle, generally four weeks long, uses aerobic weight training to help develop cardiovascular fitness, muscular endurance, and explosive power. One of the main objectives of circuit training (see Chapter 4) is to teach the athlete that the point of psychological exhaustion can be pushed back, thereby permitting the entire body to be brought closer to actual exhaustion. Essentially, circuit training is training in which the athlete works with maximum effort for short periods, with short rests between exercises. The circuit of exercises is in an order which stresses different muscle groups in turn, so that, despite fatigue, the trainee is able to continue his workout. As a pre-season conditioner, circuit training with weights supplements the regular weight program. For two weeks, the athlete uses circuit training 2 times a week; for the second two weeks, just prior to the start of the competitive season, he uses it 3–4 times a week. Circuit training, as a strenuous workout, may be administered to a team or an individual in 20 minutes.

In-Season Cycle. The goal of the in-season cycle is to maintain the strength fitness developed during the off-season cycle, not to improve it. The program followed may be either circuit training or the regular individual type. In either case, the training session should not last longer than 20 minutes. A total of six exercises is sufficient for either program, keeping the repetitions down to 8–12 in 1–2 sets.

WEIGHT TRAINING FOR STRENGTH ATHLETES

Many of today's outstanding field event performers in the shot put, discus, and hammer throw are not only successful in their speciality, but also in competitive Olympic lifting. Often a champion shot-putter is also a champion Olympic lifter. Shot-putters Gary Gubner and Al Feuerback are examples of dual title holders at the national and international level. As strength athletes, they discovered early in their career that the strength fitness acquired through Olympic lifting had a direct influence on their success in shot-putting.

Dynamic strength is developed, if you recall, only through application of the progressive overload system, and not simply by heaving a 16-pound ball or hammer. An athlete practices for the shot or other field events for refinement of technique and coordination (motor control). The muscular strength necessary for a 70-foot shot put is derived primarily from fast-moving, weight-training exercises requiring overall body speed, power, and coordination. Two exercises meeting this criterion are the snatch and the clean and jerk. These exercises develop the components of dynamic strength fitness through a wide body range which is important in the discus, shot, and hammer. Power lifting, on the other hand (bench press, dead lift, and squat), while valuable in developing basic strength, is classified as slow movement exercise and has a much smaller contribution to make in the overall physical make-up of a shot-putter. For a shot-putter to possess the physical qualities and skill to snatch 300 pounds and clean 400 pounds is far more important than to be able to dead lift 600 pounds. At the height of their careers both Gubner and Feuerback snatched 350 pounds and cleaned and jerked 450 pounds while putting the shot in excess of 70 feet.

Every strength athlete performing in a field event and striving to achieve national or international ranking should read Chapter 7, Competitive Olympic Lifting, and follow the programs outlined. Learning the Olympic lifts and training for them is not an easy task. However, the time and effort invested pays big dividends through success in the shot put or other field event.

STRENGTH TRAINING FOR WOMEN ATHLETES

For the woman athlete aspiring to excel in national or Olympic competition, strength fitness is one factor that will contribute greatly to her success. What woman athlete can honestly say that a high level of strength fitness is not an important factor in her sport whether it be crew, skiing, swimming, tennis, gymnastics, or track and field? Unfortunately, of all the factors contributing to high-level athletic performances, strength fitness is the one component in which women athletes are most frequently deficient.

This deficiency can be attributed to a number of reasons. First, female participation in strength-training activities has long been discouraged due to social and cultural stereotypes which consider such participation a departure from the "traditional role." As a result, while in high school or college, women are not exposed to the same strength-training programs as men. The female is given little opportunity to develop the upper body in any strength-type activity, and is therefore often much weaker than the male, even when strength is expressed relative to body size. Also, the physiological advantages to be gained by women through strength-training activities have never been clearly understood by physical educators or coaches. No medical or scientific rationale exists for restricting the normal female from strength training; there are many reasons to encourage such participation.

Women who are motivated towards pursuing athletic excellence have some catching up to do. They will have to overcome a number of myths regarding strength training that perhaps prevent them from starting in the first place.

The most common myth is that the female who weight trains will acquire bulk muscle which is characteristic of male strength athletes. From a biochemical standpoint, this is unlikely. The male hormone, testosterone, appears to control the increase in body size and muscle bulk [12, 13, 14]. Since the plasma concentrate of testosterone is considerably higher in normal men than in normal women, it is highly probable that women will never obtain the muscle size of men.

It is another myth that the female does not possess the same physical qualities to respond to strength training as the male. Again, there is no scientific truth in this. While it is a fact that the female has less muscle mass (than males) per unit of body weight and bone density and does not possess the same absolute strength potential as the male, she can develop strength relative to her own physical potential.

Wilmore [15], in assessing the effects of a 10-week weight training program on strength in men and women, found both groups made significant gains. Women exhibited the greatest relative increase in leg and bench press strength. Of particular interest was that the final absolute value in leg strength for women was similar to the initial value for men. When the leg strength values were expressed relative to body weight, the resulting ratios were nearly identical for the two groups. Related to the lean body weight, the leg-strength values were actually higher for women! If it were not for the fact that women normally have a smaller proportion of muscle relative to a considerably larger amount of adipose (fatty) tissue (28 percent of the female body is fat as compared to 11 percent for the normal male) they would be as strong as men.

Thus it appears that Wilmore's findings indicate that the quality of muscle (the ability to contract and exert force) is the same in the male and the female and that no differences exist between the ability of the two sexes to develop muscle strength. The task facing women athletes is simply one of adopting the scientific principles of strength-fitness training presented here. Strength-fitness training is a long-term project calling for a personal commitment of many years and many long hours of hard work in a weight room. There are no short cuts nor easy exercise programs to follow. Strength training on guided weight machines brings very limited results. Only conventional weight-training exercises and programs involving the progressive overload principle will produce maximum strength fitness.

In general, the women athlete requires a progressive weight-training program that emphasizes the acquisition of basic strength and power in large muscle groups: legs, hips, lower and upper back, shoulders and arms. Following the completion of the six-month strength-building program suggested here, a more specialized year-round program can be developed around the three seasonal training cycles previously outlined. Before beginning this strength program carefully read Chapters 3 and 7.

Basic strength program for women athletes

Monday–Thursday	Reps.	Sets	Tuesday–Saturday	Reps.	Sets
Bench Press	2–5	4	Squat	2–5	4–6
Incline Press	2–5	4	1/2 Squat	1–3	4
Latissimus Pull	8–10	3	Toe Raise	8–12	3
Dumbbell Curl	8–10	3	Back-hyperextension	8–10	2
Power Clean	2–5	5	Sit-up	8–12	2
Sit-up (with weight)	8–12	3	Flexibility Exercises–10 minutes		
Flexibility Exercises–10 minutes					

Note: For the bench and incline press, squat, and dead lift to count as a repetition the training weight must be 80 percent of maximum or better.

Women who participate in strength sports—shot put, discus, javelin—should give serious consideration to learning and training on the power snatch, power clean, and high pulling movements (Chapter 7). The same training program should then be followed as that suggested for the male strength athlete with the exception of the two Olympic lifts which are replaced by power snatching and cleaning.

ISOKINETIC TRAINING

Isokinetic training is a relatively new concept in resistive exercise. Coaches and trainers believe that this type of exercise is an efficient and effecive method of strength training [16, 18, and 19]. For the strength athlete, isokinetic exercise can be an important supplementary form of exercise in developing muscular strength and muscular endurance. A variety of drastic claims have been made however, for isokinetic exercise, which have yet to be substantiated through established research procedures. In fact, the available published research is unclear regarding the superiority of isokinetic exercise over isotonic exercise in strength development [17 and 20].

Concept of isokinetic training

The basic concept of isokinetic training is that the muscle is loaded maximally through its full range of movement. This is achieved by regulating the velocity of movement so that resistance is in ratio to the force through every degree of the full range of movement. In other words, isokinetic exercise compels a muscle to contract at a maximum force at all times.

To accomplish this, an external means of stabilizing the velocity of body movement must be provided. An isokinetic training device, such as the Cybex dynamometer (see Chapter 1), inhibits acceleration while providing the mechanical means of receiving the maximal muscular force (torque) throughout the full range. The Cybex consists of a lever against which the exerciser pushes and pulls in extension and flexion and which always produces the same amount of force (resistance) that had been exerted against it. Thus, we have defined the term accommodation-resistance exercise. Energy is not spent on controlling velocity and may be concentrated on developing force.

Isokinetic versus isotonic training

In comparing isokinetic training to isotonic training there are a number of significant differences worth considering. In isokinetic exercise there is a constant load on the muscles throughout the full range of movement. This is not true in isotonic exercise. For example, in performing the two arm curl, the initial contractile force of the biceps overcomes the inertia of the weight being lifted. The ballistic action, however, imparted to the weight at the start of the curl movement, moves it through the remaining range of motion with little or no work by the contracting bicep muscles. When executing the curl, one can see that the bicep muscles are loaded only at the beginning of flexion and again at its conclusion. On the extension part (down stroke) the biceps are not working at all unless resistance is given to the gravitational pull on the weight. In Olympic lifting, technique and velocity of the body limbs in overcoming the inertia of the weight play important roles in performance. In isokinetic exercise, these factors are of little or no consideration. While isokinetic exercise is dynamic training, all ballistic action is eliminated, the load is constant, and the speed of the contracting muscles will vary with the force applied. Maximal muscle contraction can be maintained at all times. This must be considered the most distinguishing feature of isokinetic exercise.

SELECTED WEIGHT EXERCISES FOR VARIOUS SPORTS

In designing the weight training program, one should adhere closely to the procedures outlined in Chapter 3. Following are exercises recommended for 25 sports and activities on the scientific basis of: (a) mechanical analysis of the muscular movement involved in the sport or activity, (b) development of strength in major and specific muscle groups involved in the movement, and (c) development of strength through the full range of movement. From the selection of exercises, training routines can be developed to meet individual needs.

BASEBALL

Incline press
Power clean
Upright row
Triceps extension
Bent-arm pullover
Good morning exercise
Regular squat
Sit-up twisting
Dumbbell swing

BASKETBALL

Bench press
Power clean
Upright row
Dumbbell curl
Lat machine
Lateral arm raise
Bent-arm pullover
Dumbbell swing
Regular squat
Toe raise
Leg curl
Knee extension
Sit-up twisting

FOOTBALL

Bench press
Standing press
Power clean and jerk
Dumbbell curl
Lat machine
Shoulder shrug
Stiff-leg dead lift
Dumbbell swing
Back hyperextension
Regular squat
Knee extension
Sit-up twisting
Neck flexion and
  extension

GOLF

Incline press
Power clean
Upright row
Barbell curl
Dumbbell curl
Parallel bar dip
Stiff-leg dead lift
Dumbbell swing
Regular squat
Hack squat
Sit-up twisting

GYMNASTICS

Incline press
Standing press
Power snatch
Upright row
Dumbbell curl
Lat machine
Parallel bar dip
Triceps extension
Lateral arm raise
Dumbbell swing
Back hyperextension
Hack squat

HOCKEY

Incline press
Power clean
Upright row
Dumbbell curl
Lat machine
Parallel bar dip
Triceps extension
Shoulder shrug
Good morning exercise
Dumbbell swing
Hack squat
Knee extension
Sit-up twisting
Neck flexion and
  extension

MOUNTAIN CLIMBING

Incline press
Upright row
Barbell curl
Lat machine
Triceps extension
Shoulder shrug
Stiff-leg dead lift
Hack squat
Toe raise
Leg curl
Knee extension
Sit-up

ROWING

Bench press
Power clean
Upright row
Lat machine
Dumbbell curl
Parallel bar dip
Bent-arm pullover
Good morning exercise

Back hyperextension
Regular squat
Hack squat
Sit-up

SKIING

Incline press
Upright row
Dumbbell curl
Lat machine
Triceps extension
Parallel bar dip
Shoulder shrug
Good morning exercise
Dumbbell swing
Hack squat
Knee extension
Leg curl
Toe raise
Sit-up twisting

SOCCER

Incline press
Power clean
Bent-over row
Barbell curl
Parallel bar dip
Bent-arm pullover
Stiff-leg dead lift
Dumbbell swing
Regular squat
Knee extension
Sit-up twisting
Neck flexion and
  extension

SWIMMING

Back Stroke

Press behind neck
Incline press
Upright row
Lat machine
Lateral arm raise
Shoulder shrug
Dumbbell swing
Hack squat
Knee extension
Horizontal leg raise

Breast Stroke

Bench press
Power clean
Upright row

Lat machine
Triceps extension
Bent-arm pullover
Dumbbell swing
Back hyperextension
Hack squat
Leg curl
Horizontal leg raise

Butterfly

Bench press
Press behind neck
Power clean
Lat machine
Triceps extension,
    using lat machine
Bent-arm pullover
Dumbbell swing
Hack squat
Leg curl
Horizontal leg raise

Free Style

Bench press
Standing press
Upright row
Bent-over row
Triceps extension
Parallel bar dip
Bent-arm pullover
Stiff-leg dead lift
Back hyperextension
Hack squat
Horizontal leg lift

TENNIS

Incline press
Standing press
Upright row
Dumbbell curl
Reverse curl
Triceps extension
Lateral arm raise
Shoulder shrug
Stiff-leg dead lift
Dumbbell swing
Hack squat
Sit-up twisting

TRACK AND FIELD

Discus and Shot Put

Bench press
Incline press

Standing press
Power clean
Barbell curl
Tricep extension
Good morning exercise
Dumbbell swing
Regular squat
Knee extension
Sit-up twisting

Distance Running

Bench press
Power clean
Upright row
Dumbbell curl
Stiff-leg dead lift
Hack squat
Straight-arm pullover
Toe raise
Sit-up twisting

High Jump

Incline press
Bench press
Power clean
Dumbbell curl
Bent-arm pullover
Hack squat
Knee extension
Toe raise
Sit-up

Hurdling

Incline press
Power clean
Bent-over row
Lat machine
Dumbbell swing
Hack squat
Toe raise
Knee extension
Leg curl
Sit-up twisting

Javelin

Incline press
Standing press
Power clean
Triceps extension
Bent-arm pullover
Shoulder shrug
Hack squat
Toe raise

Leg curl
Knee extension
Sit-up twisting

Long Jump

Incline press
Power clean
Dumbbell curl
Triceps extension
Bent-arm pullover
Hack squat
Knee extension
Horizontal leg raise

Pole Vault

Bench press
Incline press
Power clean
Upright row
Lateral arm raise
Bent-arm pullover
Shoulder shrug
Back hyperextension
Hack squat
Sit-up twisting

Sprinting

Bench press
Power clean
Dumbbell curl
Good morning exercise
Back hyperextension
Hack squat
Leg curl
Knee extension
Toe raise

WRESTLING

Bench press
Standing press
Power clean
Bent-over row
Dumbbell curl
Lat machine
Triceps extension
Parallel bar dip
Good morning exercise
Back hyperextension
Regular squat
Knee extension
Sit-up twisting
Neck flexion and
    extension

REFERENCES

1. "The Champions Speak Out." *Physical Power* **5**:19 (December 1964).

2. Davis, E. C., G. A. Logan, and W. C. McKinney. *Biophysical Values of Muscular Activity.* Dubuque, Iowa: Wm. C. Brown Co., 1965.

3. Morehouse, L. E., and A. T. Miller. *Physiology of Exercise.* St. Louis: C. V. Mosby Co., 1963.

4. McCloy, C. H. "The Mechanical Analysis of Motor Skills," in W. R. Johnson, ed., *Science and Medicine of Exercise and Sports.* New York: Harper and Brothers, 1960.

5. Jesse, J. P. "Strength Development for Runners." *Physical Power* **6**:8–12 (December 1964).

6. Morehouse, L. E., and P. L. Rasch. *Sports Medicine for Trainers.* Philadelphia: W. B. Saunders Co., 1963.

7. Logan, G. A. "Weight Training in the Prevention and Rehabilitation of Joint Injuries." Report of Symposium, American College Sports Medicine, *Journal of the Association for Physical and Mental Rehabilitation* (July–August 1961).

8. Adamson, G. T. "Circuit Training." *Ergonomics* **2**:183–186 (February 1959).

9. DeLorme, T. L. "Restoration of Muscle Power by Heavy Resistance Exercise." *Journal of Bone and Joint Surgery* **27**:645–667 (October 1945).

10. O'Shea, J. P. "Neil Steinhauer, The Colossus of the Emerald Empire." *Strength and Health* **34**:26–28 (October 1966).

11. Steinhaus, A. H. "Strength from Morpurgo to Muller—A Half Century of Research." *Journal of the Association for Physical and Mental Rehabilitation* **9**:147–150 Sept.–Oct., 1955).

12. Johnson, L., and J. P. O'Shea. "Anabolic Steroid: Effects on Strength Development." *Science* **164**:957–959 (1969).

13. O'Shea, J. P., and W. Winkler. "Biochemical and Physical Effects of Anabolic Steroid in Competitive Swimmers and Weightlifters." *Nutrition Reports International* **2**:351–362 (1970).

14. Johnson, L. C., G. Fisher, L. J. Silvester, and C. C. Hofheins. "Anabolic Steroid: Effects on Strength, Body Weight, Oxygen Uptake, and Spermatogenesis Upon Mature Males." *Medicine and Science in Sport* **4**:43–45 (1972).

15. Wilmore, Jack H. "Alterations in Strength, Body Composition and Anthropometric Measurements Consequent to a 10-Week Weight Training Program." *Medicine and Science in Sport* **6**:133–138 (1974).

16. Thistle, H. G., Hislop, H. J., Moffroid, M., and E. M. Lowman. "Isokinetic Contraction; A New Concept of Resistive Exercise." *Archives of Physical Medicine* **48**:279–282 (1967).

17. Rosentsivley, J. and M. Hinson. "Comparison of Isometric, Isotonic and Isokinetic Exercise by Electromyograph." *Archives of Physical Medicine and Rehabilitation* **53**:249–250 (1972).

18. Councilman, J. E. "Isokinetic Exercise . . . A New Concept in Strength Building." *Swimming World* **10**:4, 5, 15 (1969).

19. Hislop, H. J., and J. J. Perrine. "The Isokinetic Concept of Exercise." *Physical Therapy* (journal of the American Physical Therapy Association) **47**:114–117 (1967).

20. Rodgers, K. L., and R. A. Berger. "Motor-unit involvement and tension showing maximum, voluntary concentric, eccentric, and isometric contractions of the elbow flexors." *Medicine and Science in Sports* **6**:253–259 (1974).

competitive
olympic lifting

INTERNATIONAL COMPETITION

Olympic lifting is widely practiced throughout the world and is especially popular in eastern Europe. Approximately 85 countries are members of the International Weightlifting Federation (IWF), the governing body of the sport. Weightlifting has been a competitive sport in the Olympic Games since the inception of the modern games at Athens in 1896. Competition at that time was confined to two lifts: the one-arm clean and jerk, and the two-arm clean and jerk. In 1896 the winning lift in the heavyweight class for the two-arm clean and jerk was 245 pounds; today bantamweights snatch this much, and the super-heavyweight record is well in excess of 550 pounds!

Between the 1896 and 1932 Olympic Games the types of lifts contested varied from two to five. Finally, at the 1932 games held in Los Angeles, three lifts were adapted for competition: the two-hand press, snatch, and the clean and jerk. For the next forty years these lifts were standard for all national and international competition. Following the conclusion of the 1972 Munich Olympic Games, however, the IWF voted to eliminate the press from further competition. Several reasons prompted this decision— judging the press had become too controversial, and its exclusion from competition gave the sport greater spectator appeal by reducing the time required to conduct a contest.

In addition to Olympic Games competition, a world championship is staged each year. Between 1946 and 1956, the United States dominated international competition. Since 1957, however, the Russians have monopolized the world championships in both the team and individual events.

GREAT AMERICAN LIFTERS

During the "golden years" of American lifting (1946–1956), Olympic and world champions like Pete and Jim George, Ike Berger, Tommy Kono, Stan Stanczyk, John Davis, Chuck Vincie, and Norbert Schemansky set the present world standards for style and technique in competitive lifting. In the 1950s this group of athletes completely dominated Olympic and world lifting records. Tommy Kono alone, during an illustrious career spanning some 15 years, established and re-established 28 world records while winning two Olympic titles and nine world titles. Kono richly deserves being called America's greatest strength athlete.

◄ **Fig. 7.1** Joe Puleo, National AAU Champion and Pan American Champion in the 181-lb class, in a solid jerk position.

Fig. 7.2 Norbert Schemansky snatching a world record of 363 lbs in 1962.

◄ **Fig. 7.3** Schemansky lifting the famous Apollo railroad wheels in Paris, in 1954. The wheels weigh 363 lbs and are connected by a nonrevolving shaft which has a circumference of 7½ inches.

No other athlete has had a more profound effect on split lifting than has the "grand master" Norbert Schemansky. Repeatedly, he demonstrated that a split-lifter could be as effective as a squat-lifter and proved it by setting many national and world records. With an athletic career spanning 30 years, and including one Olympic title and three world titles, Schemansky set snatching records in the middleheavyweight class (319 lbs. in 1951) and the heavyweight class (374 lbs. in 1962) that are still considered outstanding by today's standards.

STRENGTH FITNESS FOR OLYMPIC LIFTING

The development and training of a young strength athlete to become a quality Olympic lifter involves much more than just drilling him in the correct lifting techniques. National and international competition today demands almost total development of the four basic components of strength fitness (muscular strength, endurance, flexibility, and coordination) plus aerobic power (Chapter 1). Therefore, the prospective strength athlete must bring all of his physical energies to bear on the acquisition of a combination of muscular strength fitness and aerobic power.

Explosive dynamic strength and power is acquired through a variety of both fast-moving and slow-moving strength-building exercises. Fast-moving exercises include dead-hang power snatches and power cleans, high pulls, and regular snatches and cleans using 90 percent or more of maximum from the floor position. Slow-moving exercises are squats, dead lifts, and functional isometrics.

Flexibility is one component of strength fitness that is often overlooked. Good flexibility of muscles and tendons allows them to respond properly to the stresses and strains of violent contractions which occur in Olympic lifting. Static stretching movements yield the desired training results safely (see Chapter 8 for flexibility exercises).

Coordination for Olympic lifting is achieved through a combination of strength, flexibility, and many hours of practicing correct technique. If flexibility is poor, coordination is poor. Without strength, good coordination will be lacking for a maximum lifting effort. Improvement in overall coordination can be obtained through gymnastics, especially floor exercises.

Muscular endurance is the component of strength fitness that permits maximum strength performance to occur over an extended period of time (for example, a four-hour weightlifting meet). Muscular endurance is dependent upon both the levels of strength and aerobic power; the stronger a muscle is the longer it can continue to function near maximum capacity. This is true, however, only if the nutritional demands of the muscle tissues are being met and the waste products of contraction are swiftly removed. To meet the increased nutritional demands of the muscle during training and competition, a reasonable level of aerobic power is essential, that is, a level that permits the lifter to recover rapidly following (1) training workouts, (2) competition, and (3) maximum lifts during workouts, and more importantly during competition.

Competition places an extra burden on the endurance capacity of an athlete. Frequently, in a contest that has many contestants long delays between individual lifts are not unusual, and so consequently a lifter must continuously warm up to maintain a competitive sensitivity for maximum lifting. Too, aerobic power is of special importance when a lifter is taking his first attempt after everyone else is finished. In this situation he is lifting alone with very little rest between attempts. To cope with such physically demanding situations, it is imperative to have a reasonable level of aerobic power.

Display of strength, flexibility, and coordination. (Courtesy of *Strength and Health*)

For the competitive Olympic lifter, the minimum amount of training required to develop and maintain a reasonable level of aerobic power is 15 minutes of running four times per week or 45 minutes of strenuous cycling three times per week. If these activities are to have any training effect on the cardiovascular-circulatory system, a heart rate of 150 beats per minute must be maintained during the running and 130–140 beats per minute while cycling. In terms of training distance this means that the athlete will be running a minimum of two miles or cycling 12 miles each workout. (See Chapter 9 for running and cycling programs.)

From an overall strength fitness standpoint, the lifter has more to gain in muscular endurance and power through cycling than from any other form of aerobic training. For the cycling to be of full value the lifter should actually become a competitive rider. That is, cycling actually becomes an intricate part of the lifters overall training program and not just a short term affair. Cycling will assist the athlete in developing maximum strength fitness without accumulating unnecessary body fat (fat contains no muscle tissue); this makes it possible for the athlete to mature physically while maintaining a stable lean body weight.

TECHNIQUES OF OLYMPIC LIFTING

Learning the proper skills for Olympic lifting should begin with thorough mastery of the correct mechanical principles. Any other approach yields only slow progress at best, possibly just failure. Practice of incorrect techniques guarantees only that one will *not* master the correct ones and that inefficiency of movement is inevitable. The correct principles are outlined in this section.

Olympic press

While the Olympic press has been eliminated from competition a brief description is presented here as it is still an excellent exercise for developing shoulder and arm power for jerking. The press involves four basic movements:

Starting layback position (Fig. 7.4a).   Upon cleaning the weight to the chest, the lifter assumes the layback position. In this position the body is evenly "bowed" from the ankles to the shoulders. The thighs and buttocks are semicontracted but the knees are not locked; if they were, the even "bow" position could not be achieved.

Initial drive (Fig. 7.4b).   Coordinating the arm and shoulder drive with a strong contraction of the thighs, buttocks, and abdomen, the lifter straightens the body and thrusts the bar toward the overhead position. Throughout the press, he maintains strong leverage by keeping the bar directly in line with the balls of the feet.

Second layback (Fig. 7.4c).   As his initial drive is propelling the bar overhead, the lifter reverts to the layback position (the even "bow" position) by thrusting the hips forward and using them as a wedge to force the weight up.

Recovery and finish (Figs. 7.4d-e).   As the bar nears the height of the pressing movement, the lifter leans into the bar by withdrawing the hips and thighs and stands erect as the press is finished.

Special practice exercises to increase pressing power are: (1) incline presses, (2) push presses, (3) dips on parallel bars; and (4) functional isometric training.

The snatch and clean

The mechanical analysis presented here for the snatch and clean (and the jerk) was prepared by Dave Webster for *Strength and Health* [1]. Mr. Webster, who is the best-known weightlifting coach in Scotland, has based his theories on the mechanics of the "quick lifts" (snatch and clean) or scientific study and detailed film analysis of performances by champions.

Starting position (Fig. 7.5a).   The head is held up, thighs are above the horizontal position, and the back is in an arched position on an average of 16–25 degrees. Placing of the hands is very wide towards the collars in

(a)

(b)

(c)

(d)

Fig. 7.4 Ohuchi, of Japan, the former middleweight world record holder for sequence pressing: (a) starting layback position, (b) initial drive, (c) second layback, (d) recovery, (e) finish. (Courtesy of *Strength and Health*)

(e)

the snatch and, for the clean and jerk, shoulder width or slightly wider. The feet (Fig. 7.6a) are pointed to the front and approximately hip breadth apart. In this position the feet are set at the strongest pulling position. When the feet are turned severely outwards (Fig. 7.6g), the knees are pulled inwards as the pull is started and are therefore placed in a bad mechanical position. When the feet are placed too far apart and the toes turned out, it is possible that when the lifter completes the pull and leaps into the split, the front foot may go forward and too far to the side. The rear foot will also go backward and to the side. As the lifter lands under the bar, his base will be diagonal and as he pushes his front knee over the toes of the front foot, the body will travel forward and sideways as it is lowered. This will offset the barbell to one side and the lifter will automatically stop lowering the body under the bar in an effort to check the bar from travelling sideways out of control. Therefore, it is important to concentrate on starting with the feet in the correct position.

First movement (Fig. 7.5b).   The first movement of the bar from the floor to the knees is due mainly to leg action and the raising of the head, shoulders, and hips simultaneously, while the back has either maintained or slightly increased its angle. This initial pull is slow. Do not attempt to speed it up by bending the arms and jerking the bar off of the floor.

Figure 7.5c (incorrect)—Avoid at all costs keeping the hips fixed and rotating the body upwards and backwards when extending the body.

Figure 7.5d—As the bar passes the knees, the hips are swung vigorousy forward and upwards toward the bar and a great effort must be made to keep the head and shoulders a little in advance of the bar as the hips are swung forward. In Fig. 7.5d, if a line were drawn from shoulder to instep, it would be ahead of one drawn from hip joint to instep. The nearer this hip line is to being vertical, the better the lift is likely to be.

Fig. 7.5 The snatch and clean: (a) starting position, (b) initial pull, (c) incorrect initial pull, (d) hips are thrust forward and up, (e) incorrect hip position, (f) the long pull, (g) the squat snatch, or (h) the split snatch, (i) the finish. (Courtesy of *Strength and Health*)

Figure 7.5e (incorrect)—This illustrates an incorrect position in the pull.

Figure 7.5f—The lifter must apply maximum force for maximum time over maximum distance. The most efficient lifters continue pulling hard over a greater distance and for a longer time before going under the bar.

Second movement.   The second movement of the snatch and clean varies according to whether the lifter uses the squat or split technique.

Squat snatch and clean—Upon completion of his pull, the lifter jumps astride and turns his toes outwards (Fig. 7.6h) and slightly in advance of the starting position. The feet are in a position so the knees can be spread apart widely—bringing the hips forward and close to the heels—at the same time permitting the upper two thirds of the trunk to be nearly vertical. The back should be at an angle of between 60–70 degrees (Fig. 7.5g). Upon jumping into the low position in the squat, keep the bar secure and under control and drive up with the legs. When snatching, never permit the arms to unlock once they are straight. In the squat clean, keep the elbows in a fairly high position to avoid hitting the thighs.

Split snatch and clean—When the lifter has reached the completion of the pull, the forward and upward dirve of the hips earlier in the pull will cause the body to travel forward and downward when the lifter leaps into the

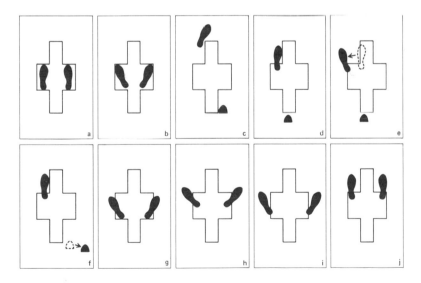

Fig. 7.6 Foot patterns of correct and incorrect lifting: (a) correct starting position; (b) incorrect starting position; (c) correct position in the split; (d) incorrect position in the split, due to backward pull; (e) incorrect position in the split, due to uneven pull on front leg; (f) incorrect position in the split, due to uneven pull on rear leg; (g) incorrect position in the squat, feet did not move from starting position; (h) correct position in squat, feet jumped to side and slightly ahead; (i) incorrect position in squat, feet jumped too far to side; (j) incorrect position in squat, feet jumped too far ahead. (Courtesy of *Strength and Health*)

split position. As the feet land simultaneously (Fig. 7.6c), the knee of the forward leg should be pushed forward over the toes of the foot traveling to the front. A fast wide split is desirable in the split style. The average of world champion lifters is about 29.9 inches from the heel of the front foot to the toe of the rear foot (Fig. 7.5h). The body is in an upright position, the thigh of the front leg below horizontal, and the knee of the front leg in a position over the toe. The rear leg should be well braced with the rear knee near the platform. The bar is locked at arm's length for the snatch or firmly fixed at the chest in the clean.

In recovering from the split position, drive off the front leg to stand erect and then push and step forward with the rear leg (Fig. 7.5i).

The jerk

After completion of the clean, the lifter should be in the following position ready to jerk the bar overhead: feet are hip width apart, elbows well in front of the bar, the bar resting on the shoulders as much as possible, and the head slightly up. After a short pause in this position, the lifter takes a short dip with the legs and then straightens them out while at the same time giving the bar a strong arm thrust driving the bar overhead and catching it at arm's length in a solid split position. (This point in the jerk is well illustrated in Fig. 7.1.) *Do not step back* when splitting. The most important part of the jerk is coordinating the leg and arm drive. If they are performed simultaneously the bar develops momentum that helps carry it overhead. In recovering from the split, the front leg is straightened and a step forward is taken with the rear leg.

Summary of Techniques Involved in the Snatch and Clean and Jerk.   In summation, the main points one should concentrate on in order to produce a correct pull and correct foot position in either the split or squat techniques are:

1.   feet pointing in the correct direction and spaced so that the legs can exert their greatest force (Fig. 7.6a),

2.   the bar lifted vertically from the floor to the knees by raising the head, shoulders, and hips simultaneously (Fig. 7.5a),

3.   as the bar passes the knees, the hips swung vigorously forward and upward toward the bar (Fig. 7.5b),

4.   the head and shoulders kept slightly in advance of the bar during the major part of the pull.

5.   at the completion of the pull, both feet taken off the floor simultaneously while maintaining an erect position of the trunk,

6.   in the split technique, when the feet land (Fig. 7.6c), the forward knee must be pushed forward over the toes of the front foot (Fig. 7.5h),

7.   in the squat technique, the feet should be jumped slightly forward and to the side with the toes pointing outward (Fig. 7.6h),

8. the jerk is a short controlled dip, a vigorous rebound combined with a strong thrust of the arms.

THE BEGINNING TRAINING PROGRAM

To develop a new trainee into an accomplished competitive lifter requires, on the average, three to four years of concentrated work. This statement is based on the premise that the prospective lifter possesses at least average physical qualifications of strength, speed, and coordination and an above-average willingness to undertake the hard work required. The main factors influencing athletic performance are: (a) constitutional build, (b) total strength fitness, (c) muscular power, (d) cardiovascular fitness, and (e) neuromuscular coordination. The early training program should emphasize developing these factors, together with the correct mechanical principles of the Olympic lifts.

When performed correctly, with precision and style, the Olympic lifts are complex movements involving a high degree of technique. Sound technique results only from a long period of practicing thousands of repetitions of the movements with light and medium weights. Each workout should begin with agility drills, stretching, jumping, and splitting exercises. Agility drills improve the athlete's ability to control his body quickly and efficiently without running the risk of injury. Following the agility drills the trainee should work on form and technique of the snatch. First, he should draw the proper foot patterns on the platform; then, using a plain bar or broomstick, he should practice the snatching movement from the dead hang position until the proper reflex movements become second nature. Later he can use weights, increasing the poundage continually as long as he can continue to perform the movement correctly with speed and precision. Only after the basic mechanics of the snatch have been learned should he proceed to the clean and jerk.

For an individual to develop proficiency of movement in the Olympic lifts with medium-heavy weights will require on the average of nine months of continuous work. This statement does not imply that the trainee has become a competitive lifter, only that he is ready for a more intensified lifting program.

Recommended training program for beginners

	Repetitions	Sets
Agility drills		
Form work on snatch		
Press—regular or incline	3–5	4–5
Power snatch or clean	2–3	4–5
High pulls from blocks on floor	2–3	4–5
Squat	2–5	5–6
Leg lunge	3–5	4–5

THE INTERMEDIATE TRAINING PROGRAM

The intermediate training period normally consists of three 3-month cycles with a week's layoff between cycles. A training program of 4 or 5 days per week is recommended. The average length of a workout is usually about 1½ hours.

(a)

(b)

(c)

(d)

(e)

Fig. 7.7 Squat snatching sequence: Walter Imahara, National AAU champion. (Courtesy of *Strength and Health*)

Fig. 7.8 Squat cleaning sequence: Bob Bednarski, National AAU champion. (Courtesy of *Strength and Health*)

Cycle 1 will stress heavy basic exercises along with technique work on the Olympic lifts. During Cycle 2, the trainee begins a combination program of functional isometrics and Olympic lifting. The intensity of the Olympic lifting is gradually increased as the lifter's overall fitness and skill improve. Both functional isometrics and Olympic lifting should be practiced twice a week. Cycle 3 is devoted almost entirely to Olympic lifting and preparing for the first contest. Practicing snatches and cleans from the blocks should play an important role in this training cycle.

THE ADVANCED TRAINING PROGRAM

The correction of deficiencies in overall strength fitness and lifting technique is the goal of a well-planned and organized advanced training program. Tommy Kono has stated, "A champion is a champion because he works on his weak points rather than specializing on his strong points. A champion keeps improving because he is willing to work on the exercises he dislikes for he knows that it is necessary."

A major mistake made by experienced lifters is to try to improve their lifting total without first making an effort to correct their deficiencies. Technical faults are magnified many times as the load being lifted increases. The complete champion is one who has recognized his faults early in his athletic career and worked diligently to overcome them. Basically, all lifting faults are related to one or more of the four components of strength fitness discussed earlier in this chapter.

As a lifter progress from the intermediate to the advanced level, he must strive to train with maximum weight (90 percent or better) to develop the neuromuscular patterns required for maximum lifting effort. Jesse [2] recommends that the experienced lifter practice hundreds of repetitions with near maximum loads to establish automatic correct "conditional reflex" patterns of lifting and also that the lifter condition the mind and emotions for the all-out effort required in international competition. Arkady Vorobiev, former Olympic champion and Russian national coach, recommends for developing a combination of strength and technique, 25 attempts each week in both the snatch and clean with 80–85 percent of maximum.

Auxiliary Training for Power and Technique

Improvement in strength and technique is also dependent upon the auxiliary exercises the advanced lifter practices. Auxiliary exercises are designed to develop power where power is most needed in Olympic lifting, in the pull. A mechanically strong correct pull is the trademark of every lifting champion. Consequently, pulling movements should constitute 85 percent of a workout, again using 90 percent of maximum or better.

TRAINING FOR THE JERK

The primary problem involved in executing the jerk is the lack of strength necessary to continue the initial drive beyond the top of the head. Frequently, we see a lifter complete a heavy clean and then fail in the jerk due to the lack of strong leg thrust or a poor lockout. An analysis of the jerk would reveal several faults or weakness common among lifters in their application of force.

After cleaning the weight, the lifter initiates the bar drive with a vigorous and simultaneous contraction of the muscles of the abdomen, hips, thighs, and buttocks followed by a short dip and then straightening of the legs, together with a strong arm thrust, all of which propels the bar over-head. At this point, the bar is caught at arm's length with the body in a solid split position. The critical factor in the entire jerk movement is the blending together of the leg drive with the shoulder and arm thrust. This must be a smooth transition. If the lifter's problems are mechanical, he must execute hundreds of repetitions to perfect his style. Otherwise, if no mechanical problems exist, improving the jerk becomes a matter of in-creasing overall body strength.

Auxiliary Jerk Exercises. The following series of exercises is designed to improve technique and develop power in the jerk.

1. *Press from the rack*

     Position 1. Press lockout (Fig. 7.9a): Starting position 3–4 inches be-low full lockout.

     Position 2. Middle press lockout (Fig. 7.9b): starting position 2–3 inches above the top of the head.

2. *Jerk lockout in the rack.* Using either Position 1 or 2 above. Assume a split position and then stand erect with the weight to the completed jerk position.

3. *Front squat and jerk.* Take the weight from the rack, perform a front squat and then jerk the weight overhead.

4. *Push jerk.* This exercise is especially beneficial in developing strength in the deltoids, triceps, abdominals, and hip flexors. Using a load close to his maximum jerk, the lifter aided by a slight "knee kick" drives the weight overhead to full arm extension.

5. *Incline press.* This is an excellent exercise for isolating and develop-ing strength in the entire upper shoulder girdle—especially the del-toids and triceps.

6. *Functional isometrics.* This type of training is valuable in developing basic strength and power for jerking. Consult Chapter 5 for a com-plete training outline.

◄ **Fig. 7.9a** Press lockout

Fig. 7.9b Middle press ►

In all auxiliary jerking exercises, the lifter strives to develop explosive power. Explosive power is the summation of the forces generated by all the muscle groups involved in the movement being performed. The inertia of the weight can be overcome only by a summation of these forces in their proper sequences: vigorous contraction of the abdominals, hip flexors, thighs, and thrust of the legs to start the jerk, followed by strong deltoid and triceps extension to complete it. As in the snatch and clean, the jerk must be executed in a strong and fluid movement.

TRAINING FOR THE SNATCH AND CLEAN (QUICK LIFTS)

Any mechanical analysis of the "quick lifts" must logically begin with an understanding of the principle of force involved. Force is the effect which one body exerts on another. Between force and motion there exists a close relationship. You may have force without motion (isometrics), but not motion without force. The outcome of a lifting contest is in most instances not determined by which lifter generated the greatest amount of "brute" force, but rather by which one harnessed the generated force and used it in the most productive manner. The secret of becoming a champion or simply improving one's performance lies in an understanding of the factors which make up the correct application of force. In the execution of the snatch or clean, the total effective force generated is the sum of the forces of the major muscle groups involved, applied in a single direction and in the proper sequence. The initial lift of the bar from the floor is an upward motion supplied by legs and trunk, which is a very powerful force; and this force will be blended, as its acceleration decreases, into the movement of the arms, shoulders, and trapezius. Quite obviously the strength of the flexion of the upper body is less than that of the lower. If there were an effort to apply all of these forces simultaneously, thereby jerking the bar off the floor, the initial pull would be so strong as to overwhelm the forces of the other groups because of the increased reaction resulting from the greatly accelerated rise of the bar. The principle of force applied here is to delay in the beginning the use of the arm and shoulder muscles until the acceleration produced by the previous force (legs and hips) has diminished to the point where the strength of the arms, shoulders, and trapezius can be applied effectively.

The Double Knee Bend Technique for Snatching and Cleaning. The most significant change in Olympic lifting technique during the past few years has been the development of the double knee bend maneuver in snatching and cleaning. This technique was developed by the Eastern European coaches in their search for maximal lifting efficiency and is presently being used by the champion lifters of Bulgaria, Poland, and Russia (see Figs. 7.10 and 7.11) with unqualified success. The following mechanical description of the double knee bend technique is based upon material provided to this writer by Carl Miller, U.S. National Weightlifting Coach.

Fig. 7.10 Rigert (Russia) using the double knee bend technique and pulling 375 lbs in the snatch. (Courtesy *Strength and Health*)

Fig. 7.11 Jenson (Norway) using the double knee bend technique and pulling 336 lbs in the snatch. (Courtesy *Strength and Health*)

(a)   (b)

(e)   (f)

Mechanical principles of the double knee bend pull

Pulling in the snatch or clean is a blending of straight forces from the floor to complete body erection. The forces must be exerted against the bar in the proper direction so far as practicable, for the total effective force in pulling is the sum of all the components of the various body forces acting in that direction. In executing the double knee bend maneuver, the sequence of movements can be divided into three phases; (1) initial pull from the floor, (2) second knee bend or "body scoop," and (3) the second pull.

First pull. The starting position has the lifter with his head up, feet shoulder width apart and pointed out slightly, and the shoulders positioned well out over the bar (Fig. 7.12a). The hips, when anatomically feasible (usually lifters having long upper thighs), are at a greater angle

(c)   (d)

(g)

Fig. 7.12 Double knee bend pull sequence.

than parallel to the floor. With the hips high, the thighs (one of the prime movers) are in a better position to exert maximum force on the initial pull. With the hips higher, the angle of the lever arm (where the bar would intersect the spine) will be decreased since the back is lower.

For the initial pull of the bar from the floor, the body weight is centered on the balls of the feet and then shifts to the middle of the feet when the bar reaches knee height (Fig. 7.12b). At the start of the second pull, the body weight will again shift back to the balls of the feet.

The first pull is explosive, that is, as fast as the body leverage permits. The movement of the legs and hips upward serves the purpose of overcoming the inertia of the weight (Newton's First Law). During the first pull, the hips are held toward the bar and move up vertically as the body and knees straighten. At this point the weight of the body must have shifted from the balls of the feet back to the middle of the feet. Continuously increasing acceleration of the bar as it moves from one phase of the pull to the next is due only to the summation of forces as each optimum leverage point is reached. This requires the lifter to pull at a velocity that permits proper body leverage to be maintained. If the bar velocity decreases at any point before the start of the second pull, the final velocity it can develop is practically always less than maximum. The sequence of movement in the pull should be such that just before one muscle group completes its action on the bar, the action of the next begins. The succession of actions must take place at an increasingly faster pace. Never attempt to rush the first pull by yanking the bar off the floor. One must maintain preception of body movement and sensitivity for the weight being lifted throughout all phases of the pull. Both are crucial factors and must be developed by the lifter if he is to learn to smoothly execute the double knee bend maneuver.

Second knee bend.   As the bar reaches a position just above the knees it is brought back about two inches while simultaneously the knees bend again (Figs. 7.12b and 7.12c). In bending the knees, the hips come forward and down, the body weight shifts from the middle of the feet to the balls of the feet with the whole foot remaining in contact with the floor. Meanwhile, the back has straightened up (Fig. 7.12c). This "scooping" action of the knees under the bar is a critical maneuver for it places the lifter in the correct position for the second pull. Bending the knees with the bar close into the thighs greatly improves the angle of pull. Consequently, the muscles of the upper back, shoulders, and arms are provided with a strong pulling base from which to work. Combining the double knee bend maneuver with the increasing momentum of the bar results in a more powerful pull.

The wrists throughout the pull are kept in a flexed position. This throws the elbows forward and out to the sides and also causes the trapezius to be stretched longer, thus having a longer pulling effect on the bar.

Second pull.   The second pull begins with the bar cradled in against the thighs and the body weight forward on the balls of the feet (Fig. 7.12c). Great acceleration of the bar will now be supplied by the second pull. It must be emphasized that the complete pulling movement from the floor to overhead in the snatch, or to the waist in the clean, is one continuous action with increasing acceleration. The second pull is started with the scooping action of the legs and hips. As these big muscles accelerate lifting the bar, the extension of the back then blends in and not before. This results in a continuation of the up motion of the bar which is further continued by the later blending in of the elevation of the shoulders. Finally, the end of the pull results in the lifter going up on his toes, body fully extended, and shoulders shrugged (Fig. 7.12d). Maximum height with maximum force has been implanted to the bar.

The sequence of exercises to practice in learning the double knee bend maneuver is: snatch grip dead lifts, high pulls from the floor and blocks beginning with a wide grip and then working towards a narrower one, power snatches and cleans from the floor and blocks, and then finally, regular snatches and cleans.

Training from blocks

For a powerful second pull to be applied effectively, mechanically correct patterns of lifting are a must. The research study comparing good lifters to champion lifters (presented at the end of this chapter) shows that the good lifter pulls the bar almost a foot higher and yet requires more time to fix the weight on the chest. The use of blocks can be of primary help in establishing or improving correct lifting techniques of snatching and cleaning. Training from the blocks eliminates a good portion of the initial force supplied by leg action, thus forcing the lifter to rely on greater co-ordination, optimum speed, and correct mechanical principles of lifting. It also requires the muscle groups of the upper body to do more of the work, thus developing a powerful second pull.

Height of Blocks.   Depending on the height of the lifter, the blocks used in training should be approximately 10 inches high. When the weights rest on the blocks, the bar should be about parallel with the knees.

Starting position (for High Pulls, Snatch and Clean, Fig. 7.13). Using the hand straps, assume the following position: feet 6–8 inches apart, knees 2 inches from the bar, shoulders ahead of the bar, head up, and the small of the back arched. Hands should assume a wide grip for snatch, narrow grip for clean.

Fig. 7.13 Correct starting position. Note that the shoulders are out over the bar and the back is in an arched position.

Initial pull.   A small portion of the force still originates in the legs; however, the hips and lower back must supply most of the lifting force. The initial pull from the blocks is strong and slow. Never attempt to rush the pull by bending the arms and jerking the bar off the blocks.

Top of the pull (Fig. 7.14).   As the bar accelerates upward, the muscles of the upper body begin to work. Again following Webster's analysis of a correct pull, "the body should be forcibly extended, thrusting the hips forward and upward. Avoid at all cost keeping the hips fixed and rotating the body upwards and backwards when extending the body."

Fig. 7.14 The top of the pull. The first part shows the wide grip which permits the high pulls to develop snatching power; the second part shows the narrow grip which permits the high pulls to develop cleaning power.

Fig. 7.15 The lifter should practice snatches and cleans to improve his technique.

Snatching and Cleaning (Figs. 7.15 and 7.16).   Snatching and cleaning from the blocks improves agility, balance, control, flexibility, and speed. It also aids in developing the powers of concentration, for the lifter must coordinate all the powerful muscles of the body to make them work in their proper sequence at the proper time. At first, the trainee should use light weights until the correct patterns of lifting become automatic and constant. Only when he has reached this point should he use heavier loads to build strength and increase maximum force. A good lifter will be able to snatch or clean from the blocks only 15–20 pounds less than his maximum from the regular starting position on the floor.

Fig. 7.16 The lifter should practice power snatches and cleans to improve his power.

Power Snatches (Fig. 7.16).   Power snatching requires the lifter to extend the body completely, to derive the maximum force from his pull through the full range of movement.

A suggested training program of 6–8 weeks for intermediate and advanced lifters

Program A

Monday and Thursday	Reps.*	Sets
Incline press (45° angle)	2–5	3–5
Power snatch or clean (alternate workouts)	2–3	4–6
High pull from blocks or floor	2–3	4–6
Jerks from rack	1–3	3–5
Flexibility exercises (8–10 minutes)		

Tuesday and Friday

Flexibility (8–10 minutes)

Technique work on the snatch and clean and jerk using 70–80 percent of maximum.

Perform the first repetition form and then two more for the dead hang position (4–6 sets).

Squats–front and back; working up in the front position to 90–100 percent of maximum and then continue on with the heavier back squats. Perform 2–5 repetitions for 6–8 sets counting only those sets in which 85 percent of maximum or better has been used.

---

* To count as a repetition the training weight must be 80 percent of maximum or better.

Program B

Monday and Thursday

Functional isometrics–see Chapter 5 for details (substituting jerk exercises for the press).
Flexibility exercises (8–10 minutes)

Tuesday and Saturday*

Snatch and clean from the blocks using 75–85 percent of floor position maximum.
Perform 8–10 repetitions in each lift.
High pulls from the floor or blocks varying the grip from the wide snatch grip moving inward towards the clean grip as the weight increases. Perform 2–3 repetitions for 5–8 sets.
Flexibility exercises (8–10 minutes)

---

* Every other Saturday go for maximum effort in the Olympic lifts.

Peaking for a Contest.   In peaking for a contest begin to taper down on the training intensity four days before competition. For instance, if the meet is to be on Saturday, in Tuesday's workout, the lifter should work up to his starting poundages in each lift, doing six singles with this weight. On Thursday, the lifter should take a short workout for technique and to maintain a feel for the weight. The lifter should not force the intensity of the workouts; there is absolutely nothing to be gained from that type of training before a contest. The athlete wants to enter the contest in a highly conditioned physical and emotional state and this is not possible if one is fatigued from over training.

ESTABLISHING TRAINING LOADS: THE K-VALUE SYSTEM

Advanced lifters face two critical problems: establishing a productive training intensity and setting a realistic two-lift contest total. These problems are interrelated; one method of solving them is through calculation of the *K*-value. The formula for determination of a *K*-value is

$$K = \frac{I_a \times 100}{TOTAL}$$

where

I_a = average weight lifted during a known number of weeks,
TOTAL = the sum of the two Olympic lifts, in pounds.

The *K*-value is a constant that supplies the relationship between the training intensity (I_a) and the *TOTAL*. In other words, it tells a lifter at what level of intensity he must work in order to achieve a realistic two-lifts contest *TOTAL*. The two-lifts *TOTAL* is based upon good judgment and experience; it is not wishful thinking or overestimation of one's capabilities.

In other words, a *K*-value reflects the intensity of training in proportion to the total. As the lifter's *TOTAL* goes up, the I_a must increase proportionally if the established *K*-value is to be maintained. Over a period of time a lifter's *K*-value may not vary greatly, while both the I_a and the *TOTAL* gradually increase. Eventually however, as a lifter is maturing physically and is lifting at a high level of performance, his threshold of training increases greatly (see Chapter 1). At this point, the lifter must work close to maximum with greater frequency in training to elicit a small increase in *TOTAL*. In short, "the law of diminishing returns" is in effect. For the world champion lifter this means that a small improvement in *TOTAL* will come only from having a very high I_a compared to his *TOTAL,* which will result in a high *K*-value. (Eastern European lifters have *K*-values of 40 and slightly higher.)

K-values are normally calculated on a monthly basis to allow for gradual upward or downward adjustment in the lifter's strength and technique. These are the factors which determine the I_a and the *TOTAL*. In peaking for a contest a lifter's *K*-value is calculated two weeks before the event. Four or five days before the meet a planned gradual tapering off of the daily I_a begins.

The average training intensity is calculated by totaling the weight lifted (only the two Olympic lifts and all pulling movements) during the set period (usually 2–4 weeks) and then dividing by the number of total repetitions. Only those lifts that are 80 percent or better of maximum are counted, including all successes and failures. The formula for determining average training intensity is

$$I_a = \frac{TOTAL\ POUNDAGE}{TOTAL\ REPETITIONS}.$$

Establishing a K-value. An initial *K*-value is established in the following manner. A lifter preparing for a contest two weeks away realistically predicts for himself a two-lift *TOTAL* of 700 pounds (300 pounds in snatch and 400 pounds in clean and jerk). During this two-week period the lifter keeps a close account of all lifts. At the end of this precontest period the training poundage totals 51,000 pounds and the repetitions add up to 200. The lifter's average training intensity (I_a) was 255 pounds ($I_a = 51,000/200$). The *K*-value for this I_a and projected *TOTAL* is

$$K = \frac{255 \times 100}{700} \approx 36.43.$$

Following the contest, if the lifter has failed to achieve the projected 700 pounds *TOTAL,* an evaluation of his performance is necessary. Either one of two factors may have contributed to his failure. The projected

TOTAL may have been set too high and must be lowered. By lowering the *TOTAL* and maintaining the same I_a, the *K*-value will increase. The other factor may have been overtraining which means that the I_a must be lowered. Lowering the I_a while keeping the same *TOTAL* decreases the *K*-value. At a lower I_a, the lifter trains at a work intensity more in keeping with his present level of strength fitness and lifting technique. Whether or not an athlete is overtraining or undertraining is pretty much a subjective evaluation, and a valid judgement can only be made by comparing the past and present performances.

If, on the other hand, the lifter was successful in totaling 700 pounds, his workouts during the next four to six weeks must be adjusted to an I_a of 255 pounds, in order to maintain the established *K*-value of 36.43. That is, training poundages and repetitions may vary but the I_a will remain at 255 pounds.

At the completion of six weeks of training, the lifter may set his next contest goal at 720 pounds. In order to maintain the same *K*-value he must readjust the I_a upward. The new I_a is calculated by

$$\text{new } I_a = \text{old } I_a \times \frac{720}{700}$$

$$= 255 \text{ lbs} \times \frac{720}{700} \approx 262$$

$$36.43 = \frac{I_a \times 100}{720}$$

or multiplying both sides by 720/100,

$$36.43 \times \frac{720}{100} = I_a.$$

So,

$$I_a = 262 \text{ lbs.}$$

With a new I_a of 262 pounds, the same relationship now exists between the training intensity and the new projected total of 720 pounds, as previously existed for the 700 *TOTAL*.

As time progresses and the lifter continues to steadily improve in strength and technique, his threshold of training will also increase. This calls for an extremely high I_a-to-*TOTAL* ratio compared to what previously existed at lower *TOTALS*. Eventually the lifter will be in the same position as the previously described champion lifter; he will have to possess all the mental and physical attributes necessary to train at a high *K*-value.

A comparison of techniques of champion lifters and good lifters

This study, conducted by researchers (3) at Michigan State University in 1958, was designed to determine the differences in technique between champion lifters (members of the United States and Soviet national teams of 1958) and good lifters (National Collegiate Champions of 1958). The results of the study should help coaches and weightlifters to see and understand what goals they should strive for in developing better technique.

To determine the difference in technique between the two classes of lifters, movies of the clean were taken in 1958 at the National Collegiate Championships and the United States–Soviet International Team Contest at Detroit. To control measurement deviation and ensure reliable interpretation, the movies were taken at identical angles, distance, and speed. Comparison and analysis were made on the basis of: (1) shoulder-drop velocity vs. free-drop velocity, (2) bar, shoulder, and hip vertical movements, (3) hip height vs bar peak height. The range of pictures extended over 12 frames of film. The average time per frame was .02 sec, so the total time measured was .24 sec.

Shoulder-drop Velocity vs. Free-drop Velocity. A body falling freely under the force of gravity accelerates at a uniform rate of 32 ft/sec/sec; that is, every second it falls its speed increases by 32 ft/sec. The velocity (V) of any free-falling body equals the acceleration provided by gravity (G) times the length of time (T) the body falls; that is, $V = GT$.

In this study, the time (T) was .24 sec, therefore $V = 32 \times .24$. So the *free-drop* velocity for the period measured was 7.7 ft/sec. But the actual shoulder-drop velocity of the lifters tested, showing the speed with which they moved under the weight and caught it at the chest, is given below:

Good lifter	Champion lifter
6.4 ft/sec	7.8 ft/sec
5.9	9.1
6.1	9.0
4.9	7.3
Ave. 5.8 ft/sec	Ave. 8.3 ft/sec

Free-drop velocity for the time measured was 7.7 ft/sec. Shoulder-drop velocity for the good lifters averaged 5.8 ft/sec, or 25 percent slower than free fall. But shoulder-drop velocity for the champion lifters averaged 8.3 ft/sec, or 8 percent *faster* than free fall. Since the champions moved faster than free-drop velocity, it must be assumed that a force besides that of gravity acted on them. This force could only be supplied by the lifter, so it seems logical to assume that they pulled themselves under the weight with great speed.

Bar, Shoulder, and Hip Vertical Movement in Cleaning. In Fig. 7.17, point A indicates the height from the floor of hip and shoulders and bar at the start of the clean. In the graph for the champion lifter, the lines for the shoulders and hips are almost parallel (point B) where the initial pull from the floor ends; this indicates that the champion lifter is deriving

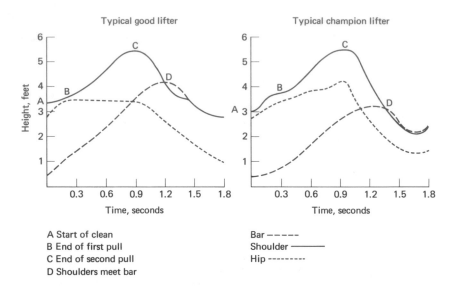

Fig. 7.17 Comparison of bar, shoulder and hip vertical movements in clean phase.

most of his initial pull from leg action and the raising of the head, shoulders, and hips simultaneously. The graph for the good lifter indicates that the legs are extending (points A to B) rapidly in comparison with the rate of rise of the bar; this suggests that the lower back was used more in the initial pull. At the end of the second pull (point C), the shoulder curve in the graph of the champion hits a sharp peak, indicating that the champion is swinging the hips upward toward the bar while the good lifter is not doing so. By extending the body properly, the champions are raising their hips at least 6 inches higher than the good lifters. The shoulders meet the bar at point (D). The graph of the champion shows that the bar does not travel above shoulder height at any time during the clean. (By shoulder height, we are referring to the height of the shoulders at the start of the clean.) The good lifter, however, is pulling the bar almost a foot higher than the champion. This indicates one of two things: the good lifter lacks either technique or the necessary leg strength to recover from the low positions.

Relationship between Hip Height and Bar Peak Height. For this part of the study, each of the two main groups of champions and good lifters were subdivided into splitters and squatters. Table I shows that the good lifters on the average were pulling the bar more than 6 inches higher than hip height. By contrast the champions were pulling the bar only to hip height. In both subgroups the squat lifters did not pull the bar as high as the split lifters. And, in two exceptional instances, it was slightly less than hip height.

TABLE 7.1   Relationship Between Hip Height and Bar Peak Height

Good lifter

Split Lifters	Hip Height (ft)	Bar Peak Height	Difference
Lahata	3.37	4.19	+ .32
Symthe	3.92	4.77	+ .85
Brason	3.51	4.23	+ .72
Total	10.80	13.19	

Squat Lifters			
Berger	3.06	3.24	+.18
Williams	3.20	4.10	+.90
Norton	3.33	3.65	+.32
Total	9.59	10.99	
Overall Total	20.39	24.18	
Mean	3.40	4.03	+.63

Champion lifter

Split Lifters			
Bushuev	3.15	3.15	.00
Bogdaovski	3.30	3.30	.00
Lomakin	3.21	3.33	+.12
Medvedev	3.63	3.96	+.33
Total	13.29	13.74	

Squat Lifters			
Kono	3.30	3.57	+.27
J. George	3.56	3.27	−.32
Shepard	3.48	3.24	−.24
Total	10.37	10.08	
Overall Total	23.66	23.82	
Mean	3.38	3.40	+.02

Summary of the Comparison. Analysis of the data revealed that the champion lifters cleaning with maximum weights had established a higher level of "conditioned reflex" patterns of automatic lifting. The champions, through greater neuromuscular coordination, used their strength to its greatest advantage. The good lifters, due to faulty technique and improperly learned conditioned reflexes, were unable to direct their strength into its most useful channels. "Strength without technique is helpless."

REFERENCES

1. Webster, D. "The Two-Hands Snatch." *Strength and Health* **32**:11, pp. 15–17 (1964).

2. Jesse, J. P. "The Role of Physical Fitness in Competitive Weightlifting." *Physical Power* **6**:6, pp. 20–23 (1965).

3. Stolberg, D. C. Unpublished master's thesis. Michigan State University, 1961.

care and treatment
of injuries related
to strength training

For a weightlifter, a muscle strain in the back, shoulder, or thigh area often means the loss of valuable training time and perhaps missing an important contest. Depending upon the nature and extent of the strain, one or two months may be required for full recovery. Ligaments strained around a joint are particularly incapacitating. Strain of the wrist, elbow, or knee require immediate and proper medical treatment and, most of all, sufficient rest. The latter is the most difficult to acquire because the urge to use the strained muscle is hard to resist.

MUSCLE STRAINS

Strains of muscle and tendons are most commonly known as pulls or tears. They usually occur at any point of the musculotendinous unit, from its origin to its insertion. The severity of the strain ranges from a tear of some fibers, as a result of overstretching, to a complete rupture of the muscle or tendon. These are classified by Novich and Taylor [1] as follows:

1. Muscle strain—tear of the body of the muscle.
2. Pulled muscle—strain or tears of the muscle near its tendinous insertion.
3. Pulled tendon—tears of tendon and its body insertion.

Martin [2] defines a strain as "a stretching, tearing, or rupture of a muscle, tendon, or fascia generally produced by a quick unbalanced muscular contraction." This is what is medically referred to as a pulled muscle. A more detailed definition of this injury is offered by Start [3]: "The so-called pulled or torn muscle occurring during exercise in healthy individuals is thought to be due to spontaneous rupture of a small number of muscle fibers. The actual lesion, however, has not been demonstrated by any direct method such as a muscle biopsy.''

Causes of muscle strain

There are many prevalent theories suggesting the cause of muscle strains. One of the most common is offered by Morehouse [4]: "The muscles most frequently torn during strenuous activity are the antagonists to the strong contracting muscles. These cold antagonistic muscles relax slowly and incompletely when the agonist contracts and thus retard free movement and accurate coordination. At the same time the forces of contraction of the agonists and the momentum of the moving part exert a terrific strain on the unyielding antagonists, with consequent tearing of the muscle fibers or their attachments." According to Slocum [5] muscle strains occur as a result of overloading either the contractile or the elastic parts of a muscle, depending at what point in the length-tension curve of the muscle the overload is applied.

A different approach to muscle strain is presented by Goldenberg [6]. "The real cause of pulled muscle is the malpositioning of the base of the spinal cord, allowing for rotation of the vertebrae which leads to pressure and mechanical stimulation of the nerves that control muscular contraction in the thigh area.''

While Goldenberg's approach to muscle injuries is academically challenging, the majority of physiologists support the more conventional theory. That is, muscle strains result when the tensile strength of the muscle or tendon fibers is exceeded by the overloading forces to which these tissues are subjected. In muscles, strains result after a vigorous contraction against resistance, as frequently happens in back injuries of weightlifters. In tendons, strain results from a force that causes overstretching, and even rupture, of a tendon at or near a point of maximal length, as seen in a split-lifter who is off balance in a deep split position. In this position, the vastus lateralis is stretched in either the front or rear leg, even leading to a severe pull of the quadricep tendon.

Muscle strain and recovery

A slight muscle strain will respond to rest and physical therapy treatments. If the strain is severe the chance of complete recovery is small. If surgery is needed, however, the muscle structure becomes inherently weakened. Severe strains not requiring surgery often heal in such a manner that some weakness remains permanently. In other words, a muscle that has suffered a severe strain frequently is not as strong as it was prior to the injury. Proper rest is critical if maximum recovery is to be expected. If a muscle is not given adequate time to rest and heal, the athlete is subject to chronic and recurrent strains and eventually arthritis. After suffering a muscle strain one must allow enough time for the healing process to complete its work before resuming strenuous training. If properly treated, a muscle strain normally will be 80 percent recovered by the end of the second week, permitting limited training. This does not mean an athlete should expect to get 80-percent efficiency from his injury after a two-week recovery period. Full restoration of the muscle takes place after a total of four or five weeks, provided one undertakes gradual resumption of hard training and also performs special remedial exercise for the injured area. An athlete must realize that it takes this long for a muscle to regain its functioning ability.

Chronic muscle strains.   No matter how much time is devoted to muscle recovery from strain, the fact remains that there are athletes faced with chronic strains. Martin [2] in commenting on chronic strains has written, "Regenerating muscle cells may not mature normally, but tend to form irregularly shaped multinucleated structures. In some cases an intermuscular hematoma is likely to organize, become encapsulated, and thus constitute a permanent lesion." This permanent lesion, which is a pathological change in the tissue, may be the cause of a chronic injury in two ways. First, it may constitute the new injury itself, the new injury being actually the tearing of the old adhesion and not the muscle itself. After such an episode, although the muscle is temporarily sore, physiotherapy and rest will produce a rapid cure.

The other possibility is that the formation of a lesion may lead to severe muscle impairment and organic degeneration. Martin [2] comments on this, too: "Some connective tissue organizing in a hematoma may undergo osseous metaplasia with the production of a lesion called *myositis ossificans*. If the injury is near the insertion of the muscle, the metaplastic bone may unite with the osseous spurs which often extend into the muscle insertion.... Fibrous-tissue repair in muscle results in weakening of this particular tissue, and therefore a tendency to reoccurrence of the strain remains."

With proper therapy, rest, and exercise chronic muscle injuries are avoided and eventually the muscle is fully capable of handling normal work loads. Just how much work and stress the repaired muscle can handle is hard to predict. When stress of an extreme overload is applied, as in competition, the strength of the muscle may not be sufficient to combat it, a breakdown may occur, and the lifter may suffer a muscle strain relapse.

Permanent damage to muscle tissue.   Permanent damage to muscle tissue may result from the following. Some athletes do not have the physiological makeup to repair torn muscle tissue adequately. The older an athlete is, the less chance there is for complete recovery. Also, failure to allow enough time for healing before the resumption of training subjects the lifter to constant stress on the injury. Each workout and competition places an extra stress upon the muscle strain. Reoccurrence of the injury drastically reduces the efficiency of the muscle and allows a degenerative process to develop within the muscle.

An athlete who is prone to muscle strains should examine carefully his dietary and training habits and lifting techniques. Flexibility is a critical factor, too, and many athletes neglect to include stretching exercises in their workouts. As a result, they become very inflexible and more susceptible to muscle strains.

FLEXIBILITY EXERCISES

Flexibility is best achieved through the overload principle and by gradually forcing the muscles and connective tissues to stretch while moving a joint through a full range of motion. In stretching one should feel the pull of the muscle but not to the point of pain.

To increase muscle flexibility two methods are commonly used— ballistic stretch and static stretch. Ballistic stretching puts a muscle in a longer-than-resting position by bouncing against the muscle in an attempt to produce greater muscle length. This method of muscle stretching can be dangerous especially if the muscle is cold. Ballistic stretching causes the muscle to tighten with the distinct possibility of tearing it.

Static stretching is the most effective and safest exercise because it stretches the muscle under controlled conditions. In a static stretch the muscle is held at a greater-than-resting length for 8–10 seconds and then relaxed for 5 seconds. This cycle of stretching and relaxing should be repeated for 5–8 repetitions in each of the following exercises.

1. Achilles Tendon Stretch (Figs. 8.1a and 8.1b). With one foot forward or with feet together, keep heels in contact with the floor and at the same time push the hips forward.

Fig. 8.1a Achilles tendon stretch   **Fig. 8.1b** Achilles tendon stretch

2. Hip Flexor Stretch (right and left hip alternate, Fig. 8.2). Pelvis is pushed forward with the pressure of the hand which is alternate of the forward leg.

Fig. 8.2 Hip flexor stretch

3. Upper-back and Neck Stretch (Fig. 8.3). In a supine position with the arms out at a 45-degree angle from the sides of the body, push down with the hands to assist raising the legs over the head. Keep knees as straight as possible.

Fig. 8.3 Upper-back and neck stretch

4. Hamstring Stretch (squatting start and finish, Figs. 8.4a and 8.4b). This is for the lumbar, spine, and posterior aspects of the hip joint. Attempt to straighten the knees as far as possible while the hands remain in contact with the floor.

Fig. 8.4a Hamstring stretch, squatting start position

Fig. 8.4b Hamstring stretch

5. Hamstring Stretch (sitting position with legs straight, Fig. 8.5).   Partner applies slow pressure (not a jerk) on the back to achieve maximum stretch.

Fig. 8.5 Hamstring stretch, sitting position

6. Advance Hamstring Stretch (Fig. 8.6).   With the legs spread, body bent straight forward at the waist, and with the hands grasping the achilles, pull the upper body forward at the waist.

Fig. 8.6 Advanced hamstring stretch

7. Adductor Stretch of the Hips (sitting position, Fig. 8.7).   Draw the feet together and close to the body and then, using the elbows, press down on the knees.

Fig. 8.7 Adductor stretch of the hips, sitting position

8. Adductor Stretch of the Hips (supine position, Fig. 8.8). In a supine position with the buttocks against a wall and with the legs raised and spread apart against the wall, rotate the feet outward while simultaneously pressing down on the thighs with the hands.

Fig. 8.8 Adductor stretch of the hips, supine position

9. Lower-back Stretch (floor position, Fig. 8.9). Using the same starting position as in Exercise 7, pull the body trunk forward and downward with the abdominal muscles.

Fig. 8.9 Lower-back stretch, sitting position

10. Lower-back Stretch (bench position, Fig. 8.10). From a seated position on a bench or chair, pull the body trunk forward and downward with the abdominals.

Fig. 8.10 Lower-back stretch, bench position

INJURY PREVENTION AND CARE*

by Bill Robertson   *Head Trainer, Oregon State University
Trainer, U.S. Olympic Team, Tokyo, 1964*

This discussion of the care and prevention of athletic injuries is not intended to be inclusive; it is primarily an outline of the most common concerns facing the athlete in a conditioning program, specifically, in a weight training program.

Much could be written about injury prevention, but the essential information is contained in a few basic preventative measures that are both advisable and valuable:

1.   Physical condition should indicate the degree of the workout. Beginners or persons in poor physical condition obviously should not attempt the workout of a highly trained, well-conditioned athlete. The beginner should study a competent text or consult a qualified person to best formulate an appropriate training program.

2.   Workout area and equipment should be adequate for the type of exercise program. Crowded conditions and equipment in poor repair may well increase the chance of injury. Carelessness and lack of attention to schedule or "horseplay" of any type should not be tolerated in workout areas.

3.   Proper warmup is an important element of injury prevention. A regular warmup should be performed before the start of every workout.

First aid procedures

Knowing the fundamental procedures of first aid can permit an athlete to minimize the time lost from his conditioning schedule in the event of an injury. It may even make it possible for him to complete his workout after he has suffered an injury.

If some injury occurs, either the athlete or a companion can apply some basic principles of first aid to ease the discomfort until someone has summoned more experienced help or a doctor. Both trainees and trainers should keep in mind that the severity of the injury can be reduced and the recovery time hastened by prompt action. No injury should be neglected—no matter how minor it may seem at the time.

When an athlete suffers any injury, he should stop the workout and take time to examine the injury so as to determine the extent of the disability. If there is any doubt as to the seriousness of the injury, he should ask for help from a trainer or physician. Until help arrives, the injured person should assume a comfortable position and should begin prompt

---

* Used by permission of the author.

treatment of the injury in accordance with the first aid procedures out-lined in the following sections.

If an athlete suffers an injury, protective measures should be applied to prevent further strain or recurrence of the injury. Such measures may include adhesive strapping, special padding, supportive braces, belts, and other aids. These aids are also discussed in the following sections.

Sprains

The immediate care of a sprain is about the same for all joints. It con-sists of cold (ice packs), compression (elastic wrap), elevation, rest, and, in the case of a severe sprain, examination by a doctor.

The joints most frequently sprained in weight training are the wrist, elbow, shoulder, low back (lumbosacral or sacroiliac), knee, and ankle.

Wrist. Most sprains of the wrist are caused by slipping or loss of balance during exercise, improper grip, lifting too great a weight, and unreason-able repetitions. Moderate sprains of the wrist usually persist for 3–7 days and severe sprains up to 2–3 weeks. This does not mean all workouts must cease, although rest is a vital part of the healing process.

Supportive wraps of adhesive tape, elastic wraps (bandage), or leather wristlets can be used to support the injured wrist so that the trainee may continue workouts. The question of workouts depends on the severity of the sprain and the amount of pain present. Adhesive strapping better con-forms to the contour of the wrist, but it requires that the area be shaved and prepared for taping and that tape be applied prior to every workout. An elastic wrap gives some support in a moderate sprain, but does not suffice in a severe sprain. Leather wristlets give a great deal of support: however, care must be taken not to apply them too tightly and thus impair the circulation.

Elbow. Sprains of the elbow usually are caused by overextension or ro-tation. Such a sprain causes pain when the elbow is either fully flexed or fully extended. Thus the elbow sprain always requires limitation of mo-tion for correct healing. Initial treatment is the same as for all other sprains, and the arm should be put at rest in a sling.

Physical therapy measures are effective in rehabilitation of the sprained elbow. When pain and swelling have subsided, the ebow can be supported by an elastic wrap applied in a figure-eight pattern and rein-forced with adhesive tape. This measure permits workouts to continue although weights should be reduced substantially.

Shoulder. Sprains of the shoulder may include damage to the tendons and musces in that area, which are closely allied with and form part of the joint capsule. Here again the initial treatment is the same; a sling should be used for support, and elastic wraps are helpful to immobilize the joint. The healing time depends upon the severity of the sprain. When a full range of motion has returned, the trainee may resume workouts, but he must reduce weights and repetitions greatly. Pain is the factor that governs the extent and amount of weight to use in recovery from a shoulder sprain.

Low back.   Low back pain commonly occurs in either of two areas: (1) lumbosacral, or (2) sacroiliac. Both injuries manifest the same symptoms except that the point of greatest tenderness for the lumbosacral sprain is a little higher on the back.

The low back injury can be incurred in many ways—lifting improperly from the floor, overhead lifting, insufficient warmup, loss of balance during workout, or trying to catch one's balance after a slip. In cases of low back injury, the injured person may experience pain or a massive muscle spasm when he leans sideways (opposite to injured side). A sacroiliac sprain may cause referred pain in the hips and legs.

Certain methods of manipulative technique are very effective in treating this condition; of course they should be attempted only by someone well schooled in these methods.

Disability from a low back injury varies greatly, from a few days' discomfort to a chronic disorder. There are belts, orthopedic braces, and supports which help in many cases, but in others, the relief they supply is only temporary. Exercises designed solely for strengthening this area and many so-called relaxation exercises have been proposed for relief of low back pain. If there is persistence of low back pain, consultation with a physician is essential, but self-determination can often do much. Methods of adhesive strapping and heavy belts help to support this area during workouts. It is not necessary to forego all physical activity because of low back pain.

Knee.   Sprains of the knee usually involve the ligaments on the inside of the knee. Rotating the knee inward with a heavy weight, slipping while attempting an overhead lift, and bouncing in a full-squat position can place too much stress on the ligaments of the knee. The controversial question of the squat or deep kneebend has been going on for some time. It is the full squat, not the half or three-quarter squat, that proves to be the real problem, for added stress is placed on the knee ligaments in bouncing erect from the full-squat position.

In knee sprains involving only ligaments, braces and supportive wraps can help support the injured part so that workouts may continue. Chronic sprains of the knee should be investigated by physicians to determine cartilage damage.

Ankle.   Ankle sprains are possibly the most irritating of all sprains and can be caused in a multitude of ways. When an ankle sprain occurs, it must be treated immediately, as in the case of all sprains. Physical therapy measures will hasten the healing process, but time for rest must be allowed so that the sprain will not become chronic. With a good program of care, a badly sprained ankle should not deter the athlete from workouts for more than a few days, but as a preventive measure, supportive taping must be applied prior to each workout. Treatments and taping should continue until all signs of sprain have gone and pain has subsided for several days.

The basket-weave type of ankle support is considered the best, but there are many variations that are adequate. Even the cloth ankle wrap in the figure-eight pattern is helpful and will prevent the recurrence of a painful sprain.

Blisters

Blisters are of great concern to all who participate in athletics. They account for as many missed workouts as severe sprains.

When a blister develops, immediate care should be taken to cleanse the area with soap and water, to sterilize with an antiseptic, and then to drain the blister by using a sterile needle, a procedure best performed by a physician. After draining, the blister area should be covered with an antiseptic ointment and taped over with a gauze pad to protect it from further irritation. Protective pads or felt "donuts" can take the pressure off the blistered area during workout periods. All blisters require careful daily care. If uncared for, they readily become infected; thus further training time is lost.

Because of the pressure created by bleeding, blood blisters under fingernails or toenails are very painful. These blisters occur frequently when the trainee changes weights. The blood blister should be cleansed thoroughly and a small hole made in the nail. Again this minor operation should be left to a physician.

Muscle tears

A tear in muscle fibers is another injury which is common in a weight training program. This is brought on by a violent contraction of the muscle, insufficient warmup, or too great a stress on a muscle.

Sometimes it shows up as a general tightening of the muscle. At its onset it may feel like a cramp, or the trainee may feel a definite pull or snap during exertion. When the muscle fibers are torn, there is an accompanying muscle spasm of all the muscles in that area; this spasm results in stiffness and pain when the torn muscle is used.

When a severe pull occurs and muscle tissue is torn, there is damage to the blood vessels and bleeding into the tissue; this must be arrested by cold packs and constriction (use of a pressure bandage). Rest is advisable to ensure healing of the torn fibers, for tears in muscle tissue can only be aggravated by continued movement.

Physical therapy treatment can be started 24–36 hours after injury or when the bleeding into the tissues has stopped. Whirlpool treatment, diathermy or wet packs, infrared heat and gentle massage are all helpful in healing this type of injury.

Once healed, the torn muscle must be carefully warmed up for a long period before workouts begin again. Pre-exercise warmup should consist of gently massaging analgesic balm into the area, a series of stretching exercises, and slowly returning into a complete extension and contraction of the muscle.

A violent contraction of a muscle sometimes presents a quick flash of extreme pain, a burning sensation, with no lasting effect or difficulty. The pain is severe for just a moment, then it is gone. This has been explained as a stretching of the muscle fibers at a point where the nerve is attached.

The muscles are covered with a substance known as facia. Often a tear or split occurs in this covering that allows the underlying muscle fiber to protrude. Upon contracting this muscle, the trainee notes that a swelling or knot appears on the surface. This is a muscle hernia. It is not serious as long as it remains small, but if it continues to grow, it should be checked by a doctor. This situation should not be confused with a hernia which sometimes appears in the lower abdominal wall—a condition generally brought about by off-balance lifting or lifting too great a weight before muscles are properly conditioned. This is an uncomfortable condition and requires the attention of a doctor.

Groin strain. This is an injury which occurs to the adductor muscles of the thigh. Fibers are torn or stretched, and bleeding into the tissue may occur where the fibers are torn, thus creating the symptoms of a muscle spasm. Although not always a painful injury, it is one that limits the athlete's movement. Initial use of cold packs and a constriction bandage and later use of physical therapy treatment help the healing process. One support that gives some relief is an elastic wrap applied to the upper leg and hip, passing around the body in the form of a belt.

Heat and massage

Injuries of some degree occur no matter how careful the athlete may be in his workout schedule. Of course, they can be guarded against, and prevention should be uppermost in the mind of the trainee. When injuries do occur, immediate care must be administered.

General muscular soreness, though not an injury, seems to be ever-present after a routine workout. What can be done to treat an injury and alleviate the muscular soreness? The two treatments most often available are heat and massage.

Heat can be applied in many forms—hot towels, electric heating pads, hot water, hot water bottles, and infrared lamps. The length of time heat should be applied is usually one-half hour for best results, though two or three applications daily may be used.

The use of massage in treating injuries or muscular soreness has several advantages: it helps to relax the muscles in the area, stimulates the circulation, helps clear the waste deposits, and lessens the soreness and discomfort. Massage should be administered with care so as not to cause additional discomfort to the patient. Given properly, massage can be of great benefit in treating injuries and helping the healing process.

CRYOKINETICS*

by Dr. Richard Irvin   *Associate Professor of Physical Education*
Oregon State University
Former Trainer, St. Louis Cardinals Football Team

Cryokinetics utilizes the combination of three physical agents which are

1. ice or other hypothermal agents,
2. massage, and
3. exercise.

The cryokinetic technique is unique in that these therapeutic physical agents are combined into a unified treatment. Although many individuals had been using variations of "ice therapy" or cryokinetics for a variety of injuries, very little had been written on the subject until Hayden [7] published the results of a study conducted at Brooke Medical Center at San Antonio, Texas in 1961. In this study, over 1,000 patients with various musculoskeletal conditions were treated with the cryokinetic procedure. In the last few years, the athletic trainers at the Universities of Illinois, Illinois State, Michigan and Oregon State, to mention only a few, have adopted the cryokinetic technique and have obtained excellent clinical results.

Cryokinetic treatment consists mainly of ice massage. The term "cryokinetic" contains in its roots the two essential components of the technique, cold and motion.

In the past, ice or other forms of cold applications had been used only as first aid measures. Utilized in this manner the beneficial effects of ice are

1. constriction of the blood and lymph vessels,
2. an anesthesia effect, and
3. retardation of general metabolism.

Gieck [8] reports that many professional baseball trainers have found it beneficial to apply ice packs to the shoulder area of pitchers just after they complete a strenuous effort. Used in this manner, the application of ice for a period of approximately 30 minutes may have a therapeutic value because it temporarily reduces the flow of blood to the strained area and thus reduces the amount of post-exercise swelling. The swelling usually occurs because of the rupturing of small blood vessels during

---

* Used by permission of the author.

violent muscular effort. The weightlifter may find it valuable to apply cold packs to those muscular areas that have been violently active during a heavy bout of training or after strenuous competition.

In the conventional method of post-injury treatment, internal hemorrhaging was controlled by cold applications, then some form of heat treatment was recommended. There has always been a great deal of disagreement among the various rehabilitationists as to when the cold treatments should be terminated and the heat treatments started. When the cryokinetic technique is employed, this particular problem is eliminated. [9] In the cryokinetic procedure, the use of cold applications is continued until healing is completed.

Moore, Nicolette, and Behnke [10] report that there are several methods by which cryotherapy may be applied. These cold applications may be in the form of

1. submersion in ice water (approximately 10–20 minutes),

2. ice packs (approximately 30–45 minutes),

3. ice massage (approximately 10 minutes), or

4. ethyl chloride spray (a series of 20-second sprays).

Massaging the affected area with ice seems to be the most effective method of application. However, in anatomical areas where irregular bone surfaces are inadequately covered by soft tissue, submersion in ice water may be the best procedure. In the massaging technique, the ice is applied directly to the skin in a very light and gentle stroking manner. In all of the methods of application, the cold treatment is terminated when the patient indicates the anatomical part is anesthetized enough to permit active pain-free exercise through a range of motion. The exact duration of the treatment is relative to several factors:

1. the type of injury,

2. the severity of the injury, or

3. the individual's physiological response to the cold application.

Downey [11] reports that when a mild cold stimulus is applied to an extremity, the response is a vasoconstriction. When the cold application is applied for a longer period of time, or if the stimulus is of a lower temperature, the response is vasodilation. It is believed that this reflex vasodilation persists long after the formal ice treatment has been completed, an effect that is in notable contrast to the termination of the therapeutic value of heat treatments once the formal heat treatment is completed. It has been hypothesized that much of the effectiveness of the cryokinetic treatment is due to

1. the reduction of muscle spasticity of the involved muscle,

2. the reflex vasodilation of the blood vessels, and

3. the anesthesia of the superficial nerves, a condition that permits pain-free movement.

The second phase of the treatment is the exercise program, which should immediately follow the ice therapy. The early initiation of an exercise program has always been an important objective of the rehabilitation program. An important fact to remember is that all of the exercises should be active, completely carried out by the patient, and not passive or stretching types of movements.

Some of the beneficial effects of this early mobilization are

1. preventing muscular atrophy and ensuring the early return of muscular strength of the injury,

2. ensuring the early return of the full range of motion of the joint, and

3. promoting circulation to the affected area, which enhances the healing of the injured tissue.

For the injured weightlifter, cryokinetics is especially helpful in treating a back, knee, or shoulder injury. It is recommended that the patient consult the appropriate medical personnel for instructions on specific exercises for rehabilitating the injured area. In general, these exercises should be both

1. isometric, to prevent loss of muscle strength or tone, and

2. isotonic, to maintain and promote joint range of motion.

The competitive weightlifter who has suffered an injury should find that cryokinetic treatment will enhance the healing of the injured tissue and permit an earlier return to competition.

Other advantages of this type of treatment are that no expensive therapeutic equipment is necessary and that the treatment is simple and safe; there is no need for extensive medication.

REFERENCES

1. Novich, M. M., and B. Taylor. *Training and Conditioning of Athletes.* Philadelphia: Lea & Febiger, 1970.

2. Martin, G. W. "Strains, Sprains, and Whiplash Injuries." *Physical Therapy Review* **39**:1202–1203 (1959).

3. Start, K. B. "Relation of Warm-Ups to Spontaneous Muscle Injury." *New York Journal of Medicine* **63**:2907–2908, 1962.

4. Morehouse, L. E., and A. T. Miller. *Physiology of Exercise.* St. Louis: C. V. Mosby Company, 1970.

5. Slocum, D. B. *Prevention Athletic Injuries.* Vol. 16, 1959. Instructional Course-Lecture American Academy of Orthopedic Surgeons, **16**:21–26 (1959).

6. Goldenburg, J. "The Real Cause of Pulled Muscles." *Scholastic Coach* **32**:32–34 (1962).

7. Hayden, Celeste A. "Cryokinetics in an Early Treatment Program." *Journal of the American Physical Therapy Association* **44**:990–993 (November 1964).

8. Gieck, Joe. "Stop it Cold!" *Scholastic Coach* **36**:1, pp. 52, 54 (September 1966).

9. Juvenal, J. P. "Cryokinetics, A New Concept in the Treatment of Injuries." *Scholastic Coach* **35**:9, pp. 40, 42, 73 (May 1966).

10. Moore, R. J., R. L. Nicolette, and R. S. Behnke. "The Therapeutic Use of Cold (Cryotherapy) In the Care of Athletic Injuries." *The Journal of the National Athletic Trainers Assoc* **2**:2 (1967).

11. Downey, John, A. "Physiological Effects of Heat and Cold." *Journal of the American Physical Therapy Association* **44**:8, pp. 713–717 (August 1964).

fitness Rx for middle age

When health is absent wisdom cannot reveal itself, art cannot become manifest, strength cannot fight, wealth becomes useless, and intelligence cannot be applied.

Herophilus
Physician to Alexander the Great

Why have a chapter on middle-age fitness in a book on strength fitness? The simple answer is that strength fitness is no longer the sole domain of youth. It is a highly prized possession that today's new "normal" middle-aged man takes pride in maintaining by participating regularly in some form of strenuous physical activity. Previously, normal middle-aged people were characterized as being overweight, and having flabby muscles, protruding abdomen, spindly legs, and poor posture. Dr. George Sheehan* describes the new normal middle-aged man as being at the top of his powers, reaching a metabolic and cardiopulmonary steady state. Strength fitness is an operational concept, a positive quality, and a vital life force. Consequently, that person is readily identified as the jogger or runner, the handball player, the cyclist, the Nordic skier, the mountain climber, and the contestant in the Master's Track and Field Championships. New normal middle-aged man symbolizes an active life-style which many admire and desire but lack the know-how to become part of. This chapter is offered for those who want to join the growing legions of new normal man. The training programs outlined are not easy; they are challenging and immeasurably rewarding for those who have the tenacity to follow them through to their conclusion.

MIDDLE AGE

From a medical viewpoint, age 35 has been arbitrarily set as the onslaught of middle age. Research, however, strongly indicates that the

---

* Dr. Sheehan is a cardiologist and distance runner from Red Bank, New Jersey, who has participated in more than a dozen Boston Marathons.

roots of middle-aged ailments have their beginnings in the late teens and early twenties. Middle age is associated with a gradual slowdown in the biological processes of the body and a reduction in human performance. For the average individual it is a time of life when virtually all vigorous physical activity ceases and he or she embarks upon a sedentary life that ultimately ends in physical bankruptcy such as obesity, heart disease, etc. The rate of middle-aged physical deterioration is generally in direct proportion to the degree of sedentarianism—the greater the degree of inactivity, the greater the rate of decay in physical fitness and health.

Mark Twain may be partially responsible for America's sedentary living habits. Twain has often been quoted as saying, "The only exercise I get is rocking on my front porch and serving as pallbearer for my dead friends who exercised." Disciples of Twain's philosophy, however, should give heed to a more contemporary writer, Dr. Thomas Cureton [1] who wrote, "The average middle-aged man in this country is close to death. He is only one emotional shock or sudden exertion away from a serious heart attack."

Attempting to clarify the term middle age is a difficult task. Physiologically, individuals age at different rates. This is attributed to genetic makeup (which is uncontrollable) and environmental factors, such as lifestyle (which are controllable). For these reasons, it is impossible to accurately assign a certain chronological age as the beginning or end of middle age. Middle age for some Americans begins in the late teens. Autopsies on 300 American soldiers (aged 18–24) who had been killed in the Korean War showed that in 77.3 percent of these cases there was gross evidence of coronary atherosclerosis [2]—a heart disease usually associated with middle age. The atherosclerosis ranged from thickening, to complete occlusion, of one or more of the main coronary arteries. A follow-up study during the Vietnam war supported the findings of the Korean study.

While individual variances exist in the aging process, there are a number of identifiable physiological changes associated with this process. Two of the most important changes take place in muscular strength and aerobic power.

Muscular strength

Research studies indicate that for the untrained individual not engaged in heavy manual labor or exercise, maximum muscle strength is reached between the ages of 18 through 20, after which it decreases gradually. Dynamometric measurements of muscle strength indicate that there is a marked reduction in strength that can be associated with disuse and increased age. Rate of decline with age in the strength of the legs and trunk muscles is greater than in the strength of the arms. This is largely attributed to the fact that the majority of people today do very little cycling, jogging, or even walking to maintain leg strength and no weight training to maintain trunk strength. Strength fitness programs, to be of any value at all, must emphasize the maintenance of these vital muscle groups.

A decline in muscular strength results in the following physiological chain reactions: (1) reduction of neuromuscular coordination, thus requiring more energy to perform a given motor task; (2) reduction of muscular endurance, or the ability of a muscle to repeat contractions; and (3) reduction in the stability of joints, especially of the knee and ankle. Loss of strength makes body joints more susceptible to injury, especially if a person is overweight.

Aerobic power

Maximum aerobic power involves the highest oxygen uptake an individual can obtain during maximal physical muscular effort for 2–10 minutes with most large skeletal muscles in action. Natural endowment plays an important role in determining maximum aerobic power, but it is greatly influenced by exercise during the ages of 10 through 20. Due to the close interrelationship between heart and lung size, cardiovascular output and the oxygen transporting system of the body, oxygen consumption is probably the best laboratory measure of a person's physical fitness, provided, of course, that aerobic power is the yardstick for determining physical fitness.

Peak aerobic power for the untrained individual is reached at 18 through 20 years of age followed by a gradual decline [3]. At age 65, the mean value is about 70 percent of what it was at the age of 25. Again, individual variations exist in aerobic power. Many middle-aged individuals who engage in strenuous aerobic activities on a regular basis have a maximum aerobic power that is higher than that found in many younger persons. The decline in aerobic power is closely tied to a decline in cardiac output in the trained as well as the untrained middle-aged individual, although the decline will be at a much slower rate in the physically fit person. Other physiological changes associated with aerobic power during middle age are: (1) systolic and mean arterial pressure begin to rise slightly; (2) blood lactate concentration is higher during submaximal exercise, but is lower during maximal exercise; and (3) heart rate reached during maximal exercise decreases (see Table 9.7). It is rare to find a heart rate of 200 or more during exercise in a physically fit middle-aged person engaging in even the most strenuous forms of physical activity.

CARDIOVASCULAR HEART DISEASE AND EXERCISE

Cardiovascular heart disease (CHD) has been designated as "Public Enemy Number 1" by the American Heart Association. CHD embraces arteriosclerosis, atherosclerosis, hypertension, stroke, and rheumatic heart disease. The factors involved in CHD, which have been identified as Coronary Risk Factors, are: heredity, hypertension, obesity, excessive smoking, stress, diabetes, high serum cholesterol, and lack of exercise. CHD is the primary cause of premature deaths among men from the ages of 25 through 65. Among women, too, the incidence of CHD is rising at an alarming rate. This rise is attributed to the increase in heavy smoking among women [4].

While all of the Coronary Risk Factors are important and deserve attention, our immediate concern will focus on the function of the heart and its response to exercise, obesity, and serum cholesterol and on sensible, challenging physical activities that can assist you in combating the degenerative diseases associated with middle age. Regular exercise, however, does not increase life expectancy. This is fixed by heredity. Regular exercise greatly improves your chances of living out a full life expectancy without being bothered by many of the common physical ailments found in individuals who live a sedentary existence.

Heart and exercise

Best and Taylor [5] state: "The heart free from disease can perform the greatest task which is ever demanded of it"; yet, one of the popular misconceptions about the relationship of the heart to exercise is the fear of developing an "athletic heart." This term implies that the beneficial enlargement of the heart which results from exercise is somehow as dangerous to health as the pathological enlargement caused by disease and sedentary living (see Figs. 9.1 and 9.2). Sensible aerobic exercise, even

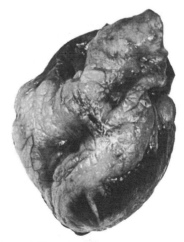

Fig. 9.1 The normal heart. (Courtesy of The Upjohn Company)

Fig. 9.2 The obese heart. Obesity results from insufficient exercise and improper diet. (Courtesy of The Upjohn Company)

during middle age, will develop a hypereffective heart, causing enlargement of the cardiac muscle and the ventricular chambers. The overall strength of the heart is greatly enhanced, and the effectiveness of the heart's pumping ability is greatly increased. Based upon his study of athletes' hearts, Wolfe [6] concluded: "As a result of training, the heart of the athlete becomes more developed, heavier and somewhat larger, as compared to the heart of the inactive individual, upon which, unfortunately, we base our concepts of norms." Wolfe's findings can be extended to include the middle-aged segment of our population.

During exercise, the heart itself needs a larger quantity of blood to flow through the coronary arteries and their branches which encircle the heart. In a normal, healthy middle-aged individual, the lining of the coronary arteries is clean and smooth. In the diseased heart, the arterial walls are thickened and rough. Supporting evidence of these statements is presented in Fig. 9.3 which shows the heart of Clarence DeMar [7], the famous long-distance runner of the 1930s and early 1940s who won the Boston Marathon seven times. His final victory came when he was 42 years old, and he competed in his last marathon at the age of 68. The

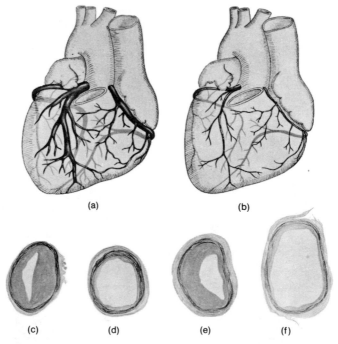

(a)   (b)

(c)   (d)   (e)   (f)

Fig. 9.3 An autopsy following his death from cancer at age 70 revealed that DeMar's coronary arteries (a) were two to three times greater in diameter than those of a normal heart (b). The main left coronary vessel (c) of the control patient who died of cancer (the normal heart) shows significant atherosclerotic narrowing of lumen. DeMar's right artery (d) shows no atherosclerosis; comparison with control (e) shows moderate narrowing of lumen in his left coronary artery (f). (Courtesy of Roche Laboratories and Roche Medical Image.)

"mint condition" of DeMar's heart at 70 years of age, as compared to the control subject, provides us with a vivid illustration as to the acute influence of regular exercise in maintaining a disease-free heart.

There are no reported cases, in the medical literature, of arteriosclerotic coronary death in anyone who has finished a marathon during the last six years. This is strong additional evidence supporting the benefits of long-term aerobic exercise, which in turn produces disease-free, healthy hearts. After finishing a four-hour marathon, a runner fits into this "protected group" of no coronary deaths. It is not the fact that the runner ran the marathon that places him in this protected group, but that he trained a minimum of one thousand miles in units of eight miles or more. Again, this illustrates the point that aerobic exercise must be a long-term affair if one hopes to benefit fully from its training effects.

Development of collateral circulation

As mentioned earlier, narrowing of the coronary arteries begins early in life; thus one of the specific reasons to exercise is to develop collateral circulation. The term "collateral circulation" means exactly what it implies, the formation of a secondary or augmentary route by which blood can flow, unrestricted, to the heart. Such circulation is dependent on anastomosis, or unions between the smaller blood vessels of the heart. When the arteries are unoccluded and functioning properly, these networks are only partially used, for the blood supply can be easily and efficiently carried by the major vessels. When the major vessels in the heart occlude, however, the collateral circulation can be developed by the inducement of exercise. The development of a collateral coronary circulation is still not fully understood, but its importance in the treatment and prevention of coronary diseases, particularly those involving blockage of a major artery, is widely acknowledged.

One researcher, Eckstein [8], has carried out exhaustive studies on the relationship of exercise to the establishment of collateral circulation in pathological hearts. Using dogs whose coronary arteries had been narrowed surgically to various degrees of occlusion and who then were subjected to exercise, he definitely established that exercise does significantly affect collateral circulation. Thus, if exercise is most effective in promoting collateral circulation when the narrowing of the coronary arteries is just beginning, we can see that the optimal time for persons to establish a program of regular exercise in order to maintain a healthy heart is at the onset of arterial occlusion, in the early twenties. Don't wait until middle age is upon you!

OBESITY AND MIDDLE-AGED SPREAD

Obesity has often been described as America's number one health problem. According to the "Build and Blood Pressure Study" [9] made in

TABLE 9.1   Smoothed Average Weights[1] for Men and Women (by Age and Height: United States 1960–62[2])

Weight (in Pounds)

Height	18–24 years	25–34 years	35–44 years	45–54 years	55–64 years	65–74 years	75–79 years
Men							
62 inches	137	141	149	148	148	144	133
63 inches	140	145	152	152	151	148	138
64 inches	144	150	156	156	155	151	143
65 inches	147	154	160	160	158	154	148
66 inches	151	159	164	164	162	158	154
67 inches	154	163	168	168	166	161	159
68 inches	158	168	171	173	169	165	164
69 inches	161	172	175	177	173	168	169
70 inches	165	177	179	181	176	171	174
71 inches	168	181	182	185	180	175	179
72 inches	172	186	186	189	184	178	184
73 inches	175	190	190	193	187	182	189
74 inches	179	194	194	197	191	185	194
Women							
57 inches	116	112	131	129	138	132	125
58 inches	118	116	134	132	141	135	129
59 inches	120	120	136	136	144	138	132
60 inches	122	124	138	140	149	142	136
61 inches	125	128	140	143	150	145	139
62 inches	127	132	143	147	152	149	143
63 inches	129	136	145	150	155	152	146
64 inches	131	140	147	154	158	156	150
65 inches	134	144	149	158	161	159	153
66 inches	136	148	152	161	164	163	157
67 inches	138	152	154	165	167	166	160
68 inches	140	156	156	168	170	170	164

[1] Estimated values from regression equations of weights for specified age groups.
[2] Adapted from National Center for Health Statistics: Weight by Height and Age of Adults, United States, 1960–1962. *Vital Health Statistics*. PHS. Publication No. 1000—Series 11, No. 14. May 1966.

1959 by the Society of Actuaries, "one in every four women and one of every five men is at least 10 percent overweight by the age of 20." Studies by the Metropolitan Life Insurance Company [10] show that average weight increases with age, increasing especially rapidly for men in their twenties and thirties.

Data on height, weight, and selected body dimensions were published recently by the National Center for Health Statistics, Public Health Service. These data, collected in 1960–62, were based on a nationwide probability sample. Thus they are more representative of the adult civilian, noninstitutionalized population in the United States than are the data from the "Build and Blood Pressure Study," which represent an "insured" population. Table 9.1 presents these new averages for men and women, by age and height.

Obesity is a difficult term to define precisely. However, we can make a distinction between obesity, which refers to fatness, and overweight, which does not carry any direct implication of fatness. There is no medical agreement on the degree of overweight which constitutes a presumption of obesity. In assessing the weight status of those they insure, insurance companies have relied upon height-weight and frame measurements. However, this method is not a reliable means of determining a desirable standard body weight because it gives no instructions for estimating body builds.

Somatotype and body weight

A reliable method of predicting and determining body weight has resulted from the research of Sheldon [11]. Somatotyping and weighing 45,000 males, ages 18 through 63, and placing them in 88 classifications, he compiled height-weight norms for each somatotype group. His weight tables project, over a 45-year period, a statistical weight trend for each somatotype. These tables make it possible to be differentially objective on the subject of optimal weight.

Briefly, somatotyping classifies the human body into types by estimating the relative predominance of inherited characteristics, namely, bone, muscle, and fat distribution. It is a subjective estimate and utilizes values from 1 to 7 with which to evaluate each of the body-type components. The three body components which Sheldon established derive their names from the three embryonic layers: The endomorph has a soft and fat body type; its name comes from the endodermic layer, the inner layer of the body which develops into the viscera or internal organs. The mesomorph is a husky and muscular individual; the term comes from "mesoderm," the middle layer of the embryo, which develops principally into muscle and bone. The ectomorph is a linear, slim person; the term comes from "ectoderm," the outer layer of the embryo, which develops into skin and nervous tissue. As you might expect, the morphological characteristics (form and structure) of all the embryonic layers are related. Thus, an individual with considerable development of the viscera rates high on the scale of the endomorphic body type. Another individual with a predominance of muscle and bone would rate high in mesomorphy, and so on. Of course, everyone possesses all the components to some degree; and for each person, each of the three components is rated on the 7-point scale, thus yielding a numerical description of the body type. For example, an individual might be described as having a body type of 2-5-3. The "2" indicates the degree of endomorphy; the "5," mesmorphy; and the "3," ectomorphy (see Fig. 9.4).

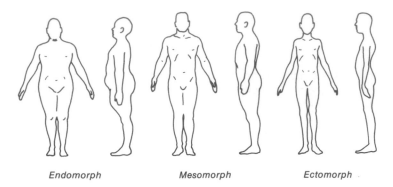

Endomorph   *Mesomorph*   *Ectomorph*

Fig. 9.4 Sheldon's somatotypes. Use this illustration and Tables 9.2 through 9.5 to determine your own somatotype. (Adapted from *Physical Activity in Modern Living,* by W. Van Huss, *et al.:* Prentice-Hall, Englewood Cliffs, New Jersey.)

Tables 9.2 through 9.5 are four weight tables selected from Sheldon's *Atlas of Men.** There is one table representative of each and one depicting the characteristics of the most common male somatotype, the 4-4-3. Using the 4-4-3 as an example (Table 9.5), we find that at a height of 69 inches, he has a mean weight of 147 pounds at college age. At 33, he has gained 22 pounds for an increase of nearly 15 percent; by the time he is 58, he will have gained another 14 pounds for a total increase of just under 25 percent of his original weight. The liability of the weight gain after age 33 is especially dangerous, for as health statistics point out, the span of 35–60 comprises the years in which men suffer the greatest number of coronary attacks.

The ectomorph has little to be concerned about with regard to weight control. However, the endomorph and mesomorph will be faced with a serious problem of weight control in the near future. Remember, though, that it is within each person's power to take preventive measures and not fall victim to obesity and its byproducts.

An individual's somatotype represents his hereditary potential as it relates to body build. Through exercise and diet, body-type changes can be realized within a limited range. Among athletes, the degree of muscle development depends in large measure on the inherited body type. For example, an extreme ectomorph could not expect to develop the heavy muscular build necessary to compete successfully as a bruising fullback or an Olympic weightlifter.

To assist in making a physical inventory, the components and characteristics of the three somatotypes are listed below. Study them and then rate yourself; then have someone else rate you. He may see you differently. Compare the ratings; this will give you a clear self-image. After

---

* Tables 9.2 through 9.5 from *Atlas of Men* (pp. 126, 132, 219, 303), by William H. Sheldon (New York, Harper & Row, 1954).

TABLE 9.2 Statistical Weight Trends for the Endomorph   6-2-2

Height (inches)	Age									
	18	23	28	33	38	43	48	53	58	63
75	223	235	246	258	268	277	280	278	277	..
74	213	225	236	248	258	266	269	267	266	..
73	205	217	226	238	248	255	258	256	255	..
72	197	208	218	228	238	245	248	246	245	..
71	189	200	209	219	229	235	238	236	235	..
70	182	192	201	211	219	226	228	227	226	..
69	174	184	192	202	210	216	219	217	216	..
68	167	176	184	193	201	207	210	208	207	..
67	159	168	176	185	192	198	200	199	198	..
66	152	161	168	177	183	189	191	190	189	..
65	145	154	161	168	175	180	182	181	180	..
64	138	146	153	161	167	172	174	173	172	..
63	132	140	146	154	159	164	166	165	164	..
62	126	133	139	147	152	156	158	157	156	..
61	120	127	132	140	145	149	151	150	149	..

TABLE 9.3 Statistical Weight Trends for the Mesomorph   2-7-1

Height (inches)	Age									
	18	23	28	33	38	43	48	53	58	63
75	228	242	250	260	266	273	273	273	272	271
74	219	233	240	250	255	262	262	262	261	260
73	211	223	231	240	245	251	251	251	250	249
72	202	214	222	230	236	242	242	242	241	240
71	194	206	213	220	226	232	232	232	231	230
70	186	197	205	212	217	223	223	223	222	220
69	178	189	196	203	208	214	214	214	213	211
68	170	181	188	194	199	205	205	205	204	202
67	162	172	178	185	189	195	195	195	194	192
66	155	165	170	177	181	186	186	186	186	184
65	148	157	163	168	173	178	178	178	177	175
64	141	150	155	161	165	169	169	169	169	167
63	134	143	148	154	157	162	162	162	161	159
62	128	136	141	147	150	154	154	154	154	152
61	122	130	134	140	143	147	147	147	146	145

determining your somatotype from Fig. 9.4, check the height-weight table that relates to your body-type classification; then plot your somatotype weight curve.

The Endomorph. Soft musculature, round face, short neck, double chin, and wide hips. Heavy fat pads distributed on the back of the upper arms, hips, abdomen, buttocks, and thighs. The trunk, arms, and the breast tend to be somewhat feminine.

TABLE 9.4   Statistical Weight Trends for the Ectomorph   3-1-6

Height (inches)	Age									
	18	23	28	33	38	43	48	53	58	63
75	153	156	158	161	165	164	161	158	..	..
74	147	150	152	155	158	157	155	152	..	..
73	141	144	146	149	152	151	149	146	..	..
72	135	138	141	143	146	·145	143	141	..	..
71	129	132	133	137	139	138	137	133	..	..
70	124	126	129	131	133	133	131	129	..	..
69	119	121	123	126	128	127	126	123	..	..
68	114	116	118	120	122	122	120	118	..	..
67	109	111	113	115	117	116	115	113	..	..
66	104	106	108	110	112	111	110	108	..	..
65	99	101	103	105	107	106	105	103	..	..
64	95	96	98	100	102	101	100	98	..	..
63	90	92	94	95	97	97	95	94	..	..
62	86	88	89	91	93	92	91	89	..	..
61	82	84	86	87	88	88	87	86	..	..

TABLE 9.5   Statistical Weight Trends for the Most Common Male Somatotype   4-4-3

Height (inches)	Age									
	18	23	28	33	38	43	48	53	58	63
75	189	198	209	217	223	231	234	234	234	234
74	181	190	201	208	214	222	224	224	224	224
73	174	183	193	200	206	213	216	216	216	216
72	167	175	185	191	197	204	207	207	207	207
71	160	168	177	184	189	196	198	198	198	198
70	154	162	170	177	182	188	190	190	190	190
69	147	155	163	169	174	180	182	182	183	183
68	141	148	156	162	167	172	174	174	175	175
67	135	142	149	155	159	165	167	167	167	167
66	129	135	142	148	152	157	159	159	160	160
65	123	129	136	141	145	150	152	157	152	152
64	117	123	130	134	138	143	145	145	145	145
63	112	118	124	128	132	137	138	138	139	139
62	106	112	118	122	126	130	132	132	132	132
61	101	107	113	116	120	124	125	125	126	126

The Mesomorph.   Solid, muscular, big-boned physique, characterized by squareness, hardness, and ruggedness. Mesomorphs are generally medium in height, possess large chests, slender waists, long torsos with relatively short, powerful legs and arms.

The Ectomorph.   Slender body, short trunk, and long legs and arms. Ectomorphs also tend to have long, narrow feet and hands, long slender necks, narrow chests, and very little fat.

The basic cause of obesity is simply overeating. Caloric intake is greater than energy expended through work or exercise, and the excess is stored as body fat. While in school, people are quite active and, as a rule, caloric intake and energy output are in balance. The problem begins when the individual leaves school and replaces an active life with a sedentary one, while retaining the old eating habits. Also, after age 20, his body becomes less efficient in its use of caloric intake. Reference to Sheldon's height-weight tables shows that the most intensive weight gain (fat gain) begins at age 23.

Among the medical profession there is a growing realization that the combination of diet and exercise is excellent preventive medicine for obesity. The problem is motivating the population to eat less and exercise more. To effect such a drastic change would require altering the living habits of millions of Americans.

Cholesterol, atherosclerosis, and exercise

Cholesterol has been identified as one of the prime factors in CHD. It is a product of animal metabolism and is therefore found in foods of animal origin, such as meat and eggs, especially egg yolks. The greater part of (body) cholesterol is manufactured within the body; however, blood serum cholesterol level can be greatly elevated through the ingestion of animal fat. Research in the past several decades has found a correlation between raised blood serum cholesterol levels and the incidence of coronary heart disease and atherosclerosis. Atherosclerosis is the deposit of cholesterol and other lipids (often called fatty plaques) in the connective tissue of the arterial walls of the heart (see Fig. 9.3). Additional factors thought to play a part in atherosclerosis include high blood pressure and sedentary living habits. Fluctuating levels of serum cholesterol and other lipids have been attributed to emotional stress, nicotine from cigarette smoking, excessive coffee drinking, and eating a few large meals a day rather than smaller and more frequent meals.

Women appear to have greater protection from atherosclerosis since the female sex hormones, the estrogens, decrease blood cholesterol whereas the male sex hormones, the androgens, increase blood cholesterol.

A review of medical literature indicates that regular aerobic exercise may be effective in reducing blood serum cholesterol concentrations and retarding the development of coronary atherosclerosis [12, 13, 14]. This is especially true when the type of physique is taken into consideration. As early as 1950 Gertler et al. [15], employing Sheldon's [11] method of physique classification, found a positive correlation between the endomorphs and high cholesterol blood levels, a negative correlation for the ectomorph, and a nonsignificant correlation for the mesomorph. The basic pattern indicated by Gertler's work shows the heavier the physique, the higher the cholesterol levels, and the more linear the physique, the lower the cholesterol levels.

Campbell [16], in studying the effects of ten weeks of running to the serum cholesterol levels of young men, found a significant reduction of cholesterol level in the subjects classified as obese, but no reduction in muscular or slim subjects. The findings of this study have far-reaching health implications when considering the fact that one in every four women and one in every five men is at least 10 percent overweight by the age of 20! One can only conclude that regular exercise and a low fat diet are essential in the struggle to prevent obesity, high concentrates of cholesterol and other lipids, and the development of atherosclerosis.

FITNESS Rx FOR MIDDLE AGE

Before committing yourself to a fitness program, every middle-aged "youth" should have a complete physical examination, preferably by a physician who practices preventive medicine and who exhibits a strong personal commitment to physical excellence (he exercises regularly and does not smoke). Such a physician will be more able to counsel the physically active middle-aged individual. A thorough physical examination will include an electrocardiogram taken under both resting and "exercise" conditions, a check for bone and joint abnormalities, blood pressure in both arms, presence of emphysema, and the level of blood cholesterol concentration. The results of the examination will provide a realistic approach to exercise with the intensity and duration suited to your physical condition at the time. You must also recognize that a physical examination does not entirely eliminate all of the risks involved in exercising.

A word of caution about exercising to those who have not been physically active for some time. Do not become too ambitious and overdo the exercising at the start. Nature will not be rushed, so there is no point in going all out on a crash conditioning program. Reconditioning a middle-aged body that has been lying around rusting over a period of years is a long-term project. Exercise at full force in the beginning will produce very negative physical and mental results. Be careful, too, to avoid unaccustomed strenuous exercise that causes a rapid rise in blood pressure (sprint running, heavy weight lifting, and isometrics), excessive overheating, and dehydration of the body. These conditions could result in cardiac arrest death. By following the progressive conditioning programs presented at the end of this chapter, the pitfalls of overexercising and underexercising will be avoided.

When it comes down to the serious business of reconditioning the body, the middle-aged individual faces a double-barreled challenge. One must first physically struggle to regain a reasonable level of muscular strength and cardiovascular fitness and then establish the discipline to maintain this level. "Reasonable" refers to a level of conditioning that allows the body to produce a given amount of work when desired with a minimum amount of physical stress.

To face life-long physical challenges and to avoid the syndrome of exercise boredom (psychological fatigue), the middle-aged person needs a variety of training programs and motivational play activities. Play is one of the basic needs of life and so any long-term physical fitness program must be developed around it. Otherwise, the self-discipline that is so essential to the success of the program soon evaporates. While discipline is the main factor in your continued participation in any physical activity, the element of play is the key to success.

Seasonal play and fitness plan

A seasonal "play and fitness" plan offers the potential of keeping your motivation towards physical fitness at a constant high level and at the same time preventing the exercise program from becoming just an end in itself. Instead, maintaining fitness becomes both fun and a challenge, flowing from one season of the year to the next. The plan takes you beyond physical fitness and focuses on playful enjoyment and the enrichment of life. It helps you grow old gracefully.

In the seasonal play and fitness plan outlined, there are both "core" fitness activities that are performed on a regular basis and seasonal "play" activities which provide the motivation to follow through with the core program (see Table 9.6). We engage in the play activities not for the extrinsic but for the intrinsic rewards (the joy of participation, fulfillment of personal needs, and the sense of achievement that comes from self-actualizing activities). This does not preclude the core activities from falling into the play category.

TABLE 9.6   Seasonal Play and Fitness Plan

Season	Core Fitness Activities	Play Activities
Summer	Cycling Swimming	Backpacking Mountaineering Tennis Scuba diving
Fall	Jogging Weight training	Backpacking Handball Squash
Winter	Weight training Jogging Swimming	Alpine/nordic skiing Ice skating Handball Water polo
Spring	Weight training Cycling Jogging	Cycle touring Tennis Golf

Strength fitness training

In Chapter 1, strength fitness was described as being a combined function of muscular strength, endurance, flexibility, and coordination. At any age these qualities are best developed and maintained through a system of progressive weight training. For the middle-aged individual, however, it is a mistake to set maximum strength development as the primary fitness goal. Remember that during the aging process muscles lose their elasticity and the use of heavy training loads may result in frequent muscle strains or even worse, pulled or torn ligaments. Middle-aged strength fitness is achieved through a weight training program that emphasizes repetitions instead of resistance (heavyweight).

To meet the strength needs of the middle-aged trainee, aerobic weight training (AWT) is recommended. Performed correctly, AWT develops and maintains all of the qualities of strength fitness and to a limited degree circulatory-respiratory fitness. AWT should be followed using the directions outlined in Chapter 4 with several exceptions. The exercising time is reduced from 45 seconds to 30 seconds and the total number of repetitions executed in each exercise is set at a minimum of 8 and a maximum of 12. Once this upper limit is reached, the exercise load may be increased but this is not necessary when the training objective is one of maintaining strength fitness. Use what feels comfortable without undue strain.

AWT exercises for the middle-aged training program are selected so that none of the major muscle groups are neglected. Target muscle groups are the shoulders and arms, body trunk, and legs. Leg exercises may be omitted if a cycling program is being followed in conjunction with the AWT. AWT is economical in time; a complete workout can be attained in as little as 20 minutes, leaving sufficient time for a 15 to 20 minute jog, bike ride, or relaxing swim.

Prior to AWT, seven or eight minutes should be devoted to flexibility movements (see Chapter 8). Flexibility exercises are designed to maintain the range of joint movements; this requires stretching of the connective tissues beyond their normal limits. Connective tissue shortens with age, and unless actively stretched, will remain shortened, thus reducing the range of motion of joints. This is especially noticeable in the shoulders and lower back. Middle-aged skiers and handball players need to concentrate on maintaining flexibility in the lower back, and the hamstrings and quadriceps of the legs.

A sample aerobic weight training workout follows:

Flexibility exercises (eight minutes for warm-up)

Weight exercises

Bench press	Supine lateral raise (concentrate on
Arm curls	deep breathing)
Latissimus pull	Sit-ups or double leg raise
Three-quarter squat to bench	

For maximum results, the circuit is repeated twice.

Aerobic fitness programs

As indicated in Table 9.6, a wide variety of aerobic conditioning activities is available. Activities such as jogging and cycling, which require relatively little in the way of skill and technique, are the most convenient means of physical self-expression in this mechanized world of ours. However, as time passes and fitness is achieved, the average middle-aged "athlete" begins to seek other means of challenging the newly found physical image. It is a general experience that we start out with jogging and then gravitate to cycling, mountaineering, cross-country skiing, etc. Lack of experience presents no barrier in learning a new physical skill once the body is reconditioned.

The remainder of this chapter describes how you can revitalize your body through jogging and cycling. Keep in mind that the programs offered are not crash programs; they will develop the mental discipline to enable you to maintain physical fitness for the remainder of your life.

Establishing a Training Pace.   One of the problems encountered by the middle-aged jogger or cyclist is establishing a training pace which will sufficiently stress the circulatory system and bring about the desired training effects. Due to individual variables, it is difficult to tell each person exactly what his training pace should be. Knowing your maximum heart rate and monitoring the exercise rate, however, will provide a good guideline for establishing and adjusting training loads to personal variables on a day-to-day basis.

Maximum pulse rate.   Maximum heart rate is the highest level attainable during maximum exercise. Heart rate is linear with increased work load and is closely tied to oxygen-uptake capacity. At any given level of O_2 uptake, the trained individual will have a lower heart rate than the untrained. During maximal exercise there is a decrease in stroke volume but the increased heart rate maintains cardiac output (the total amount of blood pumped by the heart per minute).

With age, maximum heart rate decreases. At age 25 the heart rate averages 200 beats per minute and drops about 1 beat a year up to the age of 65 (at the age of 45, maximum heart rate will be about 180). (Refer to Table 9.7.) This reduction in maximum heart rate means that maximum aerobic power is reduced and consequently the 45 year old is going to have to strain to perform the same submaximal work load which he could do easily at 25. Why this decrease in heart rate occurs is not medically known at this time.

At any given work load or O_2 uptake, the middle-aged individual attains, on the average, the same heart rate as the 25 year old; the difference being that the middle-aged individual is working closer to his maximum heart rate capacity.

Exercise pulse rate.   In comparison to the untrained heart, the trained heart has a lower initial rise in work rate during exercise, sustains a high level of output for a longer period of time without fatigue, and can perform the same amount of work at a lower heart rate. The sum total is an

TABLE 9.7 Ages and Pulse Rates

Age	Maximum	75–85 Percent
20	200	150–170
25	195	146–161
30	190	142–161
35	186	139–158
40	182	136–155
45	179	134–152
50	175	131–149
55	171	128–145
60	168	126–143
65	164	123–139
70	160	120–136

increased capacity to do endurance work which is the definition of aerobic fitness.

When establishing an effective, result-producing, aerobic training program the primary consideration is to set the intensity of the exercise to your age. For aerobic exercise to have a beneficial training effect on the cardiovascular system the heart rate should reach 75–85 percent of your age-related maximum heart rate (Table 9.7) and be maintained there for a minimum of 15 minutes. At 65–75 percent the exercise must be considerably longer. Under 65 percent the exercise is of little aerobic benefit.

The exercise pulse rate is determined in the following manner. Let us say we are going to take a three-mile training jog (not a time trial). This three-mile jog has a preset warm-up period of ¹/₂-mile which is done at a slow pace to loosen and warm the body and prepare us (mentally and physically) for the more strenuous effort ahead. Following the warm-up period, we shift gears, so to speak, and assume a faster training pace. Now, after 2–3 minutes at this faster pace we stop and take the pulse rate at the carotid artery in the neck or simply place the right hand across the breast over the heart and count the beats for 6 seconds and multiply by 10. As experience is gained in jogging or cycling, monitoring the pulse becomes unnecessary as you can fairly accurately judge your heart rate, based upon the intensity of the training pace.

Jogging.   By far the most popular and primitive physical activity of man is jogging. Less than a century ago, man relied upon his two legs for gathering food, hunting, and transportation. Contemporary man uses his legs primarily for play, games, and fitness activities. While jogging and running have fun aspects, it is work and sometimes very hard work. For the middle-aged, it is a discipline first, then play. The broad popularity of jogging may be attributed to modern man's need for strenuous physical activity. It is inherently economical in terms of equipment (only running shoes, T-shirt, shorts, and nylon windbreaker are needed), training facility (one can jog in place if necessary), and training time (an adequate workout takes only 15 minutes).

Today, physicians and exercise physiologists recognize jogging and other forms of aerobic exercise as a key factor in the practice of both preventive and rehabilitative medicine. While a long-term jogging program will greatly improve the working efficiency of the lungs, heart and circulatory system, and trim away excess body fat, it does have certain exercise value limitations. As a sole means of achieving total fitness it does not work, to a sufficient extent, the muscles of the abdomen and lower and upper back which are so important and essential for maintaining good posture. Only weight training and flexibility exercises, and to a lesser extent cycling, can effectively do this job.

Establishing a jogging program.   One of the obstacles to overcome in setting up a personalized jogging program is to select a level of exercise that is best suited to one's level of fitness. In selecting a starting point as far as exercise volume and intensity are concerned, several questions need to be answered. Most important, what was the doctor's report on your overall physical condition? And, how long has it been since you last exercised on a regular basis? If you are over 40 and have a clean bill of health from the physician but it has been quite a few years since you did

TABLE 9.8 Beginning Progressive Jog-walk Program A

10 Weeks, Poor and Below Category

Week	Monday	Wednesday	Friday	Saturday
1	½ mile	½ mile	½ mile	½ mile
2	½	½	½	¾
3	¾	¾	¾	1
4	¾	1	¾	1*
5	1	1	1	1½ mile fitness run
6	1	1¼	1	1½
7	1	1½	1	1½
8	1	1½	1	1¾
9	1¼	1¾	1¼	2
10	1½ mile fitness run	2	1½	2*

---

* Time goal (minutes expressed are for a jog-walk on the flat)

Age	1 mile	1½ miles	2 miles
25–29	10:00	14:30	18:00
30–34	10:30	15:00	19:00
35–39	11:00	15:30	20:00
40–44	11:30	16:00	21:00
45–49	12:00	16:30	22:00
50–54	12:30	17:00	23:30
55–59	13:00	17:30	25:00
60–64	13:30	18:00	27:00

TABLE 9.9   Advanced Progressive Jogging Program B

10 Weeks, Fair and Above Category

Week	Monday	Wednesday	Friday	Saturday
1	1½ miles	1½ miles	1½ miles	1½ miles
2	1½ mile fit- ness run	2	1½	2*
3	2	2	1½	2½
4	2	2½	1½	3*
5	2	2½	2	3½
6	2	3	2	4
7	2½	3	2	4*
8	2½	3	2	4½
9	3	3½	2	4½
10	1½ mile fit-	3½	2	5*
11	ness run one hour run			

---

* Time goal (minutes expressed are for jogging on the flat)

Age	2 miles	3 miles	4 miles	5 miles
25–29	16:00	23:30	31:00	40:00
30–34	16:30	24:00	33:00	43:00
35–39	17:00	25:30	35:00	46:00
40–44	17:30	27:00	37:00	49:00
45–49	18:00	29:00	39:00	52:00
50–54	18:30	31:00	41:00	55:00
55–59	19:00	33:30	43:00	58:00
60–64	20:00	35:30	45:00	61:00

anything physically strenuous, start out on the Beginning Progressive Jog-Walk Program A (see Table 9.8). This is a 10-week progressive intensity jogging program that is especially designed to meet the needs of the longtime sedentary individual. It is a program of mild intensity during which one progresses from jogging ½ mile to 2 miles in a 10-week period. Program A conditions and prepares the body for the Advanced Progressive Jogging Program B (see Table 9.9). Do not attempt to advance faster than the program rate for each week. Progress only at the given distances that are indicated each week. If a week is missed do not advance to the next. Instead, repeat the program of the previous week. Note, too, that the 1.5-mile Aerobic Fitness Test Run is not taken until the end of the fifth week. Up until this point you are not physically ready to take this test. The significance of this test is explained shortly. However, if after taking the initial aerobic test run you find yourself rated in the good category or better, you may switch over to the advanced Program B. Otherwise, continue with Program A through its conclusion.

Those who are under 40, have been training recently (within the past 6 months), and feel fairly fit may start out on the more strenuous Advanced Jogging Program B. If you start out on this program, however, and find that it is too difficult, switch over to Program A. Too, if you rate in the poor category after taking the 1.5 mile Aerobic Fitness Test Run, back down and follow Program A. By all means do not take unnecessary chances with your health by subjecting yourself to a training program that is beyond your physical capabilities. In doing so you are playing Russian roulette with your life. Those who successfully complete Program A will be physically and mentally ready for the final 5-mile jog; and for the big finale they will also have the aerobic capacity and mental confidence to tackle the one-hour run. Completing a one-hour run of 8 miles or so leaves you physically tired but one acquires a feeling of personal accomplishment and vitality that few, if any, of your middle-aged contemporaries can relate to. It is as though you had made a solo climb of Mount Everest.

1.5-Mile Aerobic Fitness Test Run. Based upon laboratory data we know that for the body to produce and maintain a set exercise rate a specific amount of oxygen is required. The purpose of the aerobic fitness test run is to measure your aerobic power; that is, the ability of the respiratory-circulatory system to deliver oxygen to the working muscles and the ability of the muscles to utilize the oxygen necessary to sustain the exercise rate. The greater the level of aerobic fitness the greater is the ability to accomplish more work (run faster) in a set time period. Or, to put it

TABLE 9.10   1.5-Mile Aerobic Fitness Test (minutes)*

Fitness Category

Age (years)	I (Very poor)	II (Poor)	III (Fair)	IV (Good)	V (Excellent)
17–29	16:30 +	14:31 to 16:30	12:01 to 14:30	10:16 to 12:00	10:15 or less
30–34	17:00 +	15:01 to 17:00	12:31 to 15:00	10:31 to 12:30	10:30 or less
35–39	17:30 +	15:31 to 17:30	13:01 to 15:30	10:46 to 13:00	10:45 or less
40–44	18:00 +	16:01 to 18:00	13:31 to 16:00	11:02 to 13:30	11:00 or less
45–49	18:30 +	16:31 to 18:30	14:01 to 16:30	11:16 to 14:00	11:15 or less
50 +	19:00 +	17:01 to 19:00	14:31 to 17:00	11:31 to 14:30	11:30 or less

* From *USAF Aerobics, Physical Fitness Program (Male),* Department of the Air Force Pamphlet 50-56, Washington, D.C., November 1969. Reprinted with permission.

another way, to perform a set amount of exercise, which in this case is running 1.5 miles in as short a time period as possible (see Table 9.10).

The purpose of the 1.5-mile Aerobic Fitness Test Run, then, is to determine your *present* capacity for performing endurance exercise. It is intended to serve as a *submaximal* test for cardiovascular endurance. This means that upon completion of the test you are not totally exhausted but could have run longer if necessary. In taking the test you run, jog, or walk depending on your physical status, but you must keep moving all the time. Based upon the results, the test will tell you which training program (A or B) to follow. Also, when taken on a test–retest basis it will indicate the degree to which you have improved over a set training period.

Dynamics of jogging. Application of the correct jogging technique is essential, otherwise improvement is retarded and injuries may occur to the foot, achilles tendon, shins (shin splints), knees, hamstrings, and lower back. Foot-fall and stride length are important if the jogger is to avoid the constant jarring of the body that occurs with the use of incorrect technique. In proper foot plant, the jogger lands first on the outside edge of the foot and rolls inward thus creating a "shock-absorber" effect. The precise point of contact along the outside edge varies with speed. In jogging, there is heel-first contact. Stride length, like foot-plant, shifts with pace; it shortens as the jogger slows or goes uphill and stretches as he speeds up. The upper body should be carried erect avoiding a forward lean. The shoulders should not rotate and the arms, with the elbows bent, hang loosely at the sides. Breathing is through the nose and mouth at a normal rate for the given pace. The breathing should not be forced.

To avoid exercise boredom which often develops when you restrict your jogging to an oval track, select a country road or a forest trail if possible. In the open country the elements of boredom and meaningless pain are absent. You can indulge your esthetic senses in the beauty of the passing countryside. When jogging, vary the gait, fast for awhile and then slow to the normal pace. Hill running and interval training should be approached with enthusiasm but only after you reach the "good" category of fitness. In interval training, you run or cycle at 90 percent of maximum (or higher) for 15 to 30 seconds, and then rest, for no longer than 90 seconds. During the rest cycle in interval training, you keep moving, but at a slow pace, to ensure good recovery before beginning the next exercise interval. This is known as the "active" recovery concept.

In the training programs which are presented in this chapter, the asterisk after a distance indicates a time trial workout. At this stage in the training program you should be physically and mentally prepared to jog or cycle the distance called for within the time set for your age group. Keep in mind that these time trials are a motivational device that will also measure your improvement. You must be able to complete the run in the time set without finishing in a state of complete physical exhaustion. After completing a time trial there should be a feeling that sufficient energy reserve remains to run faster or farther if necessary.

Cycling. Cycling is a rapidly growing middle-aged activity and one of the best means of achieving and maintaining aerobic fitness and leg strength. As a training activity, it has both advantages and disadvantages over jogging. The disadvantages include the initial cost of a bicycle (a lightweight 10-speed bicycle is necessary), problems in locating suitable locations to ride (acute traffic hazards, auto exhaust, etc.), the weather, and longer training time required for workouts (to acquire the same aerobic training effect as jogging, one has to cycle 3 to 5 times the distance). On the other hand, the advantages of cycling are increased mobility (relatively great distances can be covered in a short period of time), large muscle groups are greatly strengthened (thighs, hips, and lower back muscles), and of primary importance, because cycling is a smooth flowing movement, injuries are virtually nonexistent, provided, of course, that you do not crash. This permits you to plan out a longe-range training program with little chance of having it interrupted by an injury. Most middle-aged joggers are hampered from time to time by a variety of injuries which often result in layoffs and loss of conditioning. The older you are the longer it takes to recover from injuries, even minor ones.

Dynamics of cycling. In cycling, the application of proper techniques is paramount if the desired training results are to be achieved. Proper technique begins with a lightweight (30 pounds or under) 10-speed bicycle whose frame fits the rider's body size. Saddle height is set so that the rider's knee is slightly bent when the pedal is in the down position. Maximum leg and hip force cannot be applied to the pedals with the saddle set in a too low position. Pedal toe clips are essential, too, in deriving maximum pedal force and maintaining a high pedal RPM (especially on hills). A high pedal RPM is called "spinning" and for developing a combination of aerobic fitness and leg strength, 80–90 pedal RPMs is recommended. Gear ratio is another factor involved in pedal RPM; the higher the gear ratio the more strength is required to pedal. In training, then, select the highest gear you can possibly handle and still maintain a high pedal RPM. Until your technique and physical condition are ready for hard riding, you should start out with a smaller freewheel gear ratio (this is the rear wheel gear cluster). Do not attempt to begin with a wide-ratio freewheel.

No lengthy written description of cycling technique can totally prepare the novice of any age for the experience of riding a bicycle with maximum efficiency. The capsule description presented here, however, is sufficient to get you started in the right direction. In cycling, the weight of the body is proportionately spread between the saddle and the handlebars (45 percent of the body weight on the front wheel and 55 percent on the rear wheel). The feet are in the toe clips and the hands placed in a restful position (high or low) on the handlebars. With the hands low, the body can assume an aerodynamic position which will greatly reduce wind resistance. When accelerating on flat terrain or in hill climbing, sit back in the saddle while simultaneously pushing and pulling with the legs (applying continuous thrust on the pedals). Strive to develop a strong

TABLE 9.11 Progressive Cycling Program

10 Weeks, Fair and Above Category

Week	Monday	Wednesday	Friday	Saturday
1	1½ mile fit-ness run	8 miles	8 miles	10 miles*
2	10	10	10	12
3	10	10	10	14
4	10	12	10	15*
5	12	14	12	18
6	12	14	12	18
7	12	16	14	20
8	12	16	14	20*
9	1½ mile fit-ness run			
10	2 hour ride			

_____

* Time goal (minutes expressed are for cycling on the flat)

Age	10 miles	15 miles	20 miles
25–29	36:00	55:00	75:00
30–34	38:30	57:00	80:00
35–39	40:00	60:00	84:00
40–44	41:30	63:00	90:00
45–49	43:00	67:00	98:00
50–54	45:00	72:00	103:00
55–59	47:00	77:00	110:00

pumping action with the knees. On steep or long hills stand up and pedal when necessary. Hill training is punishing work and demands the optimum in strength, endurance, and technique. Through experience, you learn to judge the grade of a hill and shift down to a lower gear before reaching the steepest part and losing too much speed. Also, in hill riding, to allow for optimum breathing, place the hands in a high position on the handlebars and keep the head up.

Developing a mechanically sound and efficient cycling technique requires two to three months of conscientious effort (see Table 9.11). When you have obtained a riding position that feels comfortable and good progress is being made, stick with it. As technique improves, fitness will follow. In workouts use interval training at least twice a week and on long training rides try to maintain a pedal rate of 80–90 RPMs with the highest gear possible for this rate.

The Total Program. Integrating the strength fitness and the aerobic activities into one overall program requires a personal commitment of six training days a week. Initially, this may seem like an excessive amount of time to be devoting to exercising, until one considers that the average workout is only 30–40 minutes in duration. This small investment in exercising time, however, will be repaid many times over in big dividends of health, fitness, and the satisfaction of personal accomplishment.

In scheduling exercise time, set aside a definite hour of the day that allows you to be most consistent. On a tight work schedule this may require that you jog or cycle to or from work. Living 15–20 miles from work presents few problems if one can cycle. However, to jog, ride the bus to within 3–5 miles of your destination and then jog the rest of the way. While this does present some problems such as cleaning up and changing clothes (one can keep a set of clothes in the office and wash up and change in a rest room) it can and does work. One prominent U.S. Senator from the Midwest successfully followed this routine for many years. Noon hour is one of the most popular times to work out. After a morning of sedentary work, a vigorous workout serves as a good tonic to help prepare for the mental strain of afternoon work. The remaining option is to train in the evening; however, a pressing day at the office is not always conducive to the proper mood for jogging or cycling. Instead, there is a strong desire to just sit and relax with a drink and watch the evening news on TV. Based upon this writer's own experience in working with the eight-to-five business or professional man, those who wait until late afternoon or evening to exercise usually do not stick it out. Ideally, then, the best time for training is early morning or afternoon, and the following schedule presents an appropriate program for middle-aged people.

	Activity	Workout time (in minutes)
Monday	Aerobics; cycling or jogging	30–40
Tuesday	Circuit weight training and flexibility exercises	30–40
Wednesday	Aerobics; cycling or jogging	40–50
Thursday	Circuit weight training and flexibility exercises	30–40
Friday	Aerobics; cycling or jogging	30–40
Saturday	Aerobics; cycling or jogging	60–90

Training Log. Maintaining a daily training log is the best means of evaluating progress and making any necessary adjustments in the fitness program. Improvement in your level of physical fitness runs in cycles. Initially, there is rapid improvement followed by a period of regression or leveling off and then another wave of improvement. In this respect, a training log is valuable in helping to plot these up-and-down training cycles. Improvement in fitness will gradually come if you are consistent in your training and have faith in the program. Once you begin to accept excuses for missing workouts, the time is not too far off when you will "drop out" and forget about the whole idea of becoming physically fit.

REFERENCES

1. Cureton, T. K. *Physical Fitness and Dynamic Health.* New York: The Dial Press, Inc., 1965.
2. Enos, W., R. Holmes, and J. Beyer. "Coronary Disease Among United States Soldiers Killed In Action In Korea." *American Medical Association Journal* **152**: 1090–3 (1953).

3. Astrand, P. O., and K. Rodohl. *Textbook of Work Physiology.* New York: McGraw-Hill Book Co., 1970, p. 315.

4. Spain, D. M., H. Siegel, and V. A. Bradess. "Women Smokers and Sudden Death." *Journal,* American Medical Association **224**:1005–1007, 1973.

5. Best, C. H., and N. B. Taylor. *The Living Body,* 4th ed. New York: Henry Holt and Company, 1959.

6. Wolfe, J. B. "The Heart of the Athlete." *Journal of Sports Medicine and Physical Fitness* **2**:20 (1962).

7. "Physiologic Portrait of a Superathlete." *Roche Medical Image* **8**:32 (February 1966).

8. Eckstein, R. "Effects of Exercise and Coronary Artery Narrowing on Coronary Collateral Circulation." *Circulation Research* **5**:230 (1957).

9. Society of Actuaries. *Build and Blood Pressure Study, 1959,* Vols. I, II. Chicago: 1959.

10. Metropolitan Life Insurance Company. "Frequency of Overweight and Underweight." *Statistical Bulletin* **41**:4 (January 1960).

11. Sheldon, W. H. *Atlas of Men.* New York: Gramercy Publishing Company, 1954.

12. Morris, J., and M. Crawford. "Coronary Heart Disease and Physical Activity of Work." *British Medical Journal* **2**:1485–96, 1958.

13. Montoye, H. "The Effects of Exercise on Blood Cholesterol in Middle-Aged Men." *American Journal of Clinical Nutrition* **7**:139–45, 1959.

14. Campbell, D. E. "Acute Effects of Physical Activity Upon Serum Cholesterol." *The Journal of the Association for Physical and Mental Rehabilitation* **21**:87–90, 1967.

15. Gertler, M. M., S. M. Gorn, and H. B. Sprague. "Cholesterol, Cholesterol Estus, and Phosphophids in Health and in Coronary Artery Disease Morphology and Serum Lipids in Men." *Circulation* **2**:380–91, 1950.

16. Campbell, D. E. "Effects of Controlled Running on Serum Cholesterol of Young Adult Males of Varying Morphological Constitutions." *The Research Quarterly* **39**:47–53, 1968.

10

university level
strength training
courses

This chapter presents a sequence of strength-training courses which may serve as a guide in organizing and offering such activities within a university curriculum. The courses are also suitable to be offered as adult fitness courses through a YMCA or similar organization where large numbers of people would be involved. The beginning course covers the basic principles and methods of resistive exercise, the intermediate course is designed to develop a high level of aerobic power and muscular endurance, while the advanced course includes teaching the fundamentals of Olympic lifting as well as advanced methods of strength fitness.

THE BEGINNERS' COURSE

The five main objectives of an 11-week beginning weight training course are: (1) to develop overall fitness which includes strength, power, endurance, and flexibility (not to build "muscle men"); (2) to control the problem of obesity and develop weight control; (3) to prevent degenerative diseases and preserve a youthful, efficiently functioning body; (4) to find relief from emotional tensions and other nervous strains; (5) to develop a body capable of handling emergencies of everyday living and severe physical stresses that may be placed on the body from time to time.

The course outline

First week sessions

1. a. Assign students to training stations.
    b. Lecture on classroom procedures, safety rules, weight training terminology, and the basic mechanics of lifting.
    c. Class performs warm-up routines with dumbbells and barbells.
2. a. 1½-mile cardiovascular fitness test run.
    b. Class fills out the Weight Training Record Cards.

Second week sessions

1. a. Review basic lifting techniques, emphasizing the importance of correct breathing.
    b. Demonstrate and have class perform as many exercises as time permits.
    c. Assign readings from textbook.
2. a. Review exercises covered in last session.
    b. Demonstrate remaining exercises.
    c. Lecture on cardiovascular fitness.
    d. Class runs one mile.

Third week sessions

1. a. Review exercises covered in last session.
    b. Training time.
2. a. Lecture on nutrition.
    b. Assign readings from selected weight training publications.
    c. Training time.
    d. Class runs one mile.

Fourth week sessions

1. a. Begin practical testing.
2. a. Complete practical testing.
    b. Class runs one mile.
    c. Remind the students that their personal training programs are due the next period.

Fifth week sessions

1. a. Lecture on circuit training.
    b. Class performs circuit training.
    c. Collect training programs.
2. a. Training time.
    b. Class runs $1\frac{1}{2}$ miles.

Sixth week sessions

1. a. Lecture on functional isometrics and demonstrate.
    b. Circuit training.
2. a. Training time.
    b. Class runs $1\frac{1}{2}$ miles.

Seventh week sessions

1. a. Demonstrate "buddy" drills.
    b. Circuit training.
2. a. Demonstrate specialized training with dumbbells.
    b. Training time.
    c. Class runs $1\frac{1}{2}$ miles.

Eighth week sessions

1. a. Demonstrate Olympic lifting.
    b. Circuit training.
2. a. Training time.
    b. Class runs two miles.

Ninth week sessions

1. a. Training time.
2. a. Training time.
    b. Class runs two miles.

Tenth week sessions

1. a. Retest the 1½-mile cardiovascular fitness run.
    b. Training time.
2. a. Start final practical weightlifting test.

Eleventh week sessions

1. a. Complete practical test.
2. a. Administer final written exam.
    b. Collect class cards.

Outline discussion

Class Orientation. The first two class sessions are concerned with explaining the aims and objectives of the course, filling out the Weight Training Record Cards, and administering the 1½-mile cardiovascular fitness run.

Record Card. The Weight Training Record Card serves as a daily and term record of the student's progress (see Fig. 10.1). The front of the card has space for recording the 1½-mile fitness run and the practical tests. On the back of the card, the student keeps a daily training record. From this record the instructor can see at a glance the individual's progress. The class cards are meant to be kept in a wall rack where the students can pick them up at the start of each period. This system simplifies roll taking.

1½-Mile Cardiovascular Fitness Test Run. The purpose of this test is twofold: to measure the cardiovascular fitness level of the students, and by administering the test on a test-retest basis to demonstrate that healthful physiological changes can be brought about through participation in specific physical activities. (See Chapter 9 for test details.)

Assignment of Training Stations. Assignment of training stations and partners is delayed until the second class period to avoid the conflicts of late registrations and the changing of sections. Pairing of students for

DEPARTMENT OF PHYSICAL EDUCATION
WEIGHT TRAINING RECORD CARD

Name _____ *Ron Johnson* _____

Age ___*19*_____   Height _*5'11"*_____

Term _*Spring*_ Section ___*6*___   Hour _*3:00 pm*_

Instructor _____

Date	Body weight	Record of tests	Starting date *4-5*	Finishing date *6-3*	
4/5	*160*	Bench Press	*10 reps.*	*14 reps.*	
4/12	*158*	*128 lbs.*	*51*	*57*	
4/19	*157*	Curl	*8*	*13*	
4/26	*158*	*80 lbs.*	*50*	*61*	
5/3	*160*	Squat	*12*	*20*	
5/10	*160*	*160 lbs.*	*47*	*56*	
5/17	*161*	Seated Press	*6*	*8*	
5/24	*162*	*80 lbs.*	*45*	*50*	
5/30	*163*	Sit-up	*18*	*30*	
6/5	*163*	*32 lbs.*	*50*	*60*	
6/12	*164*	Parallel Bar Dip Bdy. wt.	*4*	*10*	
			36	*51*	
		TOTAL	*279*	*335*	
		AVE	*46*	*55*	

1½ - Mile Aerobic Fitness   *Improvement in*
Test Run   *Average = +9*

Date   Time

4-6   1. *12:20 - Fair*

5-4   2. *11:55 - Good*

6-3   3. *10:53 - Good*

Fig. 10.1   The weight training record card.

training is best made on the basis of equal strength. When one partner is disproportionately stronger, too much time is wasted changing weights and, more important, no spirit of competition can develop. The number of students assigned to a station depends on the size of the training facility and the amount of available equipment. Ideally, there should be two students for each station, with approximately 200 pounds of weight per station.

Lecturing.   In teaching a course in weight training, it is difficult to decide how much of a 50-minute class period to devote to lecturing. By relying on assigned readings in the text, the instructor can hold most lectures to a maximum of 10 to 15 minutes. A 5-minute class discussion on the text reading is usually sufficient to answer most questions that students may have. Following a lecture, the remainder of the class period can be used effectively in circuit training.

Running.   We should keep in mind that total fitness cannot be achieved through weight training alone. Running undoubtedly ranks high on the list of activities that develop cardiovascular fitness and control the problem of obesity. The outline requires a mile run each week. While this amount is far below minimum, it does test the student's capacity for endurance, and in most cases it serves to convince him of the need to improve his level of cardiovascular fitness.

At the conclusion of the term, the overall improvement in cardiovascular fitness will be quite evident in the final 1½-mile fitness test run.

Teaching weight training exercises

Methods of teaching these exercises will vary with the individual instructors. There are certain points, though, that need to be stressed at least once a week in beginning classes. Items that need extra emphasis are: (1) proper breathing, (2) correct lifting techniques in such basic exercises as the military press and deep knee bends, (3) the importance of following a planned training schedule instead of training haphazardly, and (4) safety. No matter how often these points are stressed, there will be students who insist on training their own way, and little can be done about it.

Aerobic Training.   Aerobic training, an indispensable tool in developing muscular endurance, also enables the instructor to discover those who are executing the exercises incorrectly. It permits a large class or group to be put through a thorough workout in a minimum of time. (For further details on aerobic training, consult Chapter 4.)

Evaluation and grading

In a beginning weight training class, evaluating is not as difficult as it may seem to be. Admittedly, in any form of evaluation there are certain inherent discrepancies. The following five criteria constitute a tested and proven system which minimizes many of the discrepancies found in other methods, such as grading on strength or improvement alone, and permits a fair and equal evaluation of each student. This testing program evaluates the student's strength fitness at the beginning and end of each term on the following bases:

1. two practical tests, administered the third and final weeks of the term,
2. improvement as indicated by the difference in the scores of the two practical tests,
3. personal attitude and interest as indicated by the class card: whether it is neat and up to date,
4. written exam based upon lectures and assigned readings,
5. performance in class: participation, attendance, etc.

TABLE 10.1   Standard Scores for Basic Weight Training Exercises

Exercises

Repetitions	Squat 100%	Sit-up 20%	Bench Press 80%	Seated Press 60%	Parallel Bar Dips 100%	Bicep Curl 50%
0	35	34	38	32	23	33
1	36	35	39	34	26	35
2	37	36	40	36	28	37
3	37	37	42	39	31	39
4	38	38	43	41	36	42
5	39	39	44	43	39	44
6	40	40	46	45	41	46
5	41	42	47	47	44	48
8	42	43	48	50	46	50
9	43	44	50	52	49	53
10	43	45	51	54	51	55
11	44	46	53	56	54	57
12	45	47	54	58	56	59
13	46	48	55	61	59	61
14	47	49	57	63	61	64
15	48	51	58	65	64	66
16	49	52	59	67	66	68
17	49	53	61	69	69	70
18	50	54	62	72	72	73
19	51	55	63	74	74	75
20	52	56	65	76	77	77
21	53	57	66	78	79	79
22	54	58	67	81	82	81
23	54	60	69	83	84	84
24	55	61	70	85	87	87
25	56	62	72	87	89	90
26	57	63	73	89	91	93
27	58	64	74	92	93	96
28	59	65	75	94	96	99
29	60	66	77	96	99	
30	60	68	78	98		

The Practical Tests.   The practical test is formed of six basic exercises that are performed with a set percentage of bodyweight for as many repetitions as possible. The six exercises and required percentages are as follows:

1.   bench press (80% of bodyweight)
2.   military press (60%)
3.   curl (back against the wall) (50%)
4.   deep-knee bend (to parallel position) (100%)
5.   sit-up (weight held behind neck) (20%)
6.   parallel bar dips (no added resistance)

TABLE 10.1 **Standard Scores for Basic Weight Training Exercises** *(cont.)*

Exercises

Repetitions	Squat 100%	Sit-up 20%	Bench Press 80%
31	61	69	79
32	62	70	80
33	63	71	81
34	64	72	82
35	65	73	84
36	65	74	85
37	66	75	86
38	67	77	88
39	68	78	89
40	69	79	90
41	70	80	91
42	71	81	92
43	71	82	93
44	72	83	95
45	73	84	96
46	74	85	97
47	75	86	99
48	76	87	
49	77	88	
50	77	90	
51	78	91	
52	79	92	
53	80	94	
54	81	95	
55	82	96	
56	82	98	

Repetitions	Squat 100%
57	83
58	84
59	85
60	86
61	87
62	88
63	88
64	89
65	90
66	91
67	92
68	93
69	93
70	94
71	95
72	96
73	97
74	98
75	99

For example, a student weighing 160 pounds is required to use 128 pounds (80 percent of his body weight) in the bench press. Using this poundage, he performs 10 repetitions. Looking up the point value for 10 repetitions of the bench press in Table 10.1, he finds that it equals a score of 51 points. He records this on his card (see Fig. 10.1), writing the exercise and weight in the column headed "Record of Tests" and the number of repetitions and points in the column headed "Starting Date." The student then performs the remaining exercises, scoring and recording them in the same manner. When he completes the test, the student totals the card and determines the average score for the six exercises. Then the instructor checks over the card, circling in red the exercises that are below the overall average of beginning students. These circles will remind the student that they signify his weak areas and that he should give special attention to improving his performance in these areas.

A quick look at Table 10.1 shows that points are given even in cases in which the student is unable to perform any repetitions with the required percentage of weight. These points are really a reward for effort; they don't substantially change his total score but they may help to keep him from being discouraged. In most such cases, the student usually improves sufficiently to be able to perform at least one or two repetitions with the correct weight on the final test.

The practical test is given once at the beginning of the sessions and again during the final week. If the student has undergone a change in body weight, he should adjust the poundages accordingly so as to be consistent in using an accurate percentage of his body weight for each exercise.

Evaluating the Class Card.   The following procedure is used: (a) points are awarded on the *average* number of total points scored on the first and second practical tests; (b) points for improvement are awarded on the *difference* between the two averages; (c) points are awarded for maintaining a neat and up-to-date class card.

Looking again at the sample record card (Fig. 10.1), we see that the average of the first practical test is 46, and of the second, 55. Checking the score on Table 10.2, we see that these averages have a respective value or score of 10 and 16. The 9-point improvement made in the average has a score of 11. The class card is fairly neat and up to date and would get 9 points on a 10-point scale.

A complete breakdown of the scoring on Ron Johnson would appear as follows:

```
First practical  ................................................ 10 points
Second practical  .............................................. 16 points
Improvement  .................................................. 11 points
Class card  .....................................................  9 points
Written examination  .......................................... 44 points*
                                                                 ——
    Total points  .............................................. 90
```

* Out of a possible 50

All scores are placed on a curve with those of the other beginning classes for final grade distribution.

In grading the class cards, the instructor always reserves the right to question any unusual improvement. A "show-me-and-I-will-believe" attitude minimizes any cheating that might take place.

At the end of a term, few education courses give an instructor the satisfaction of accomplishment that weight training does. A great amount of visual evidence exists, indicating that the students as individuals have benefited from the course. It is hoped that each student has been sufficiently stimulated to take another course in weight training or to continue with a program on his own for many years.

TABLE 10.2   Grade Points for Performance

Average on the Practical Test	—	Points Scored		Improvement in Average	—	Points for Improvement
75				16	—	15
71	—	26		15	—	14
70				14	—	14
66	—	24		13	—	13
65				12	—	13
62	—	22		11	—	12
61				10	—	12
59	—	20		9	—	11
58				8	—	10
56	—	18		7	—	9
55				6	—	8
53	—	16		5	—	7
52				4	—	6
50	—	14		3	—	5
49				2	—	4
47	—	12		1	—	3
46						
44	—	10				
43						
41	—	8				
40						
38	—	6				
37						
35	—	4				
34						
32	—	2				

THE INTERMEDIATE COURSE, AEROBIC WEIGHT TRAINING

Many students who complete the beginning course may want to continue with a weight training program but may not want to be placed in the advanced section. Their interests are best served by an intermediate class. The majority enrolling in an intermediate class are students interested in developing overall cardiovascular and strength fitness in preparation for athletics, R.O.T.C. summer training camp, or induction into the armed forces.

An intermediate weight training course should be based on the principles and guidelines established for circuit weight training in Chapter 4. The class should be scheduled for three days a week, with circuit weight training practiced on Monday and Friday. Wednesday should be reserved for individual evaluation and general workout. Each student should evaluate his own strength progress by self-testing once a week for 1-RM in the bench press and squat; and take a two-mile time trial run every other week. Practical testing and evaluating is done as in the beginning course.

In starting an aerobic weight training class, the instructor should keep in mind that the course calls for strenuous exercise and that the trainees may need several workouts to adjust themselves to it. It is strongly suggested that, to reduce the possibility of injuries, the first week or two of the course be devoted to general weight training.

THE ADVANCED COURSE

The two main purposes of an advanced weight training course are, first, to develop an appreciation for the sport of Olympic lifting, and second, to provide students the opportunity to train with more advanced methods of body building. It should not be the primary purpose of such a course to develop competitive lifters, although this may be a goal that concerns a few students. As a general rule, the caliber of student enrolling in an advanced physical education activity is extremely high. He is motivated by a strong inner urge to excel in a specialized area and is willing to put forth the necessary effort to achieve his goals. From an administrative standpoint it is important to consider this attitude when scheduling the class hour for this activity. Reserving the last class period of the day for advanced weight training provides adequate time for teaching the Olympic lifts and permits the students to extend their workouts into the after-school recreation hour.

The four main objectives of an 11-week advanced weight training course are: (1) to develop an understanding and appreciation for the sport of Olympic lifting, (2) to teach the basic mechanics and techniques of the Olympic lifts, (3) to develop an athletically functional body capable of an adequate performance in the Olympic and power lifts, (4) to increase overall physical fitness, especially strength, through the application of advanced methods of weight training.

The outline which follows is designed for an 11-week advanced weight training course. Instruction in the techniques of the Olympic lifts should be based on the methods outlined in Chapter 7.

The course outline

First week sessions

1. a. Administer $1\frac{1}{2}$-mile cardiovascular fitness test run.
   b. Class fills out record cards.
   c. Discussion of term's work.
2. a. Lecture on classroom procedures and safety regulations.
   b. Review basic principles of weight training.
   c. Have students outline their training programs on forms provided in the text. Assignment due next class period.
   d. Class runs one mile.

Second week sessions

1. a. Film on Olympic lifting.
   b. Review latest scientific research in strength development.
   c. Collect training outlines.
2. a. Return training outlines.
   b. Check students on their technique in the bench press.
   c. Class runs one mile.

Third week sessions

1. a. Check students on their technique in the squat.
   b. Assign reading on the snatch.
2. a. Demonstrate technique of both the split and squat styles of snatching.
   b. Class executes basic split patterns without weight.
   c. Class runs one mile.

Fourth week sessions

1. a. Review technique of the snatch.
   b. Class executes snatch with bar only, then slowly progresses with weight.
2. a. Review and work on snatch.
   b. Discuss and demonstrate functional isometrics.
   c. Class runs $1\frac{1}{2}$ miles.

Fifth week sessions

1. a. Continue work on snatch.
   b. Demonstrate use of block in developing strong pull and refining techniques.
2. a. Lecture on nutrition and strength development.
   b. Assign reading on clean and jerk.
   c. Class runs one mile.

Sixth week sessions

1. a. Demonstrate technique of the split and squat styles of the clean.
2. a. Review clean and jerk.
   b. Class runs $1\frac{1}{2}$ miles.

Seventh week sessions

1. a. Check on overall progress in the quick lifts.
   b. Demonstrate use of block in developing strength and technique in the quick lifts.
2. a. Training time.
   b. Class runs two miles.

Eighth week sessions

1. a. Film on power lifting.
   b. Training time.

2. a. Lecture on cardiovascular fitness and strength development.
    b. Class runs two miles.

Ninth week sessions

1. a. Training time.
2. a. Training time.
    b. Class runs two miles.

Tenth week sessions

1. a. Administer final practical test for the snatch.
    b. Class runs three miles.
2. a. Administer final practical test for the clean and jerk.

Eleventh week sessions

1. a. Readminister 1½-mile cardiovascular fitness test run.
2. a. Administer final written examination.

Evaluating the advanced lifter

In designing an evaluation system, the instructor must consider the knowledge, skill, and strength that his class has acquired concerning the Olympic and power lifts. Therefore, an evaluation system for an advanced weightlifting course must be based on the following criteria: (1) a practical skill test that measures the ability to execute the Olympic lifts with a reasonable amount of weight, (2) a written examination covering lectures and assigned readings and the knowledge to design a weight training program.

Where school policy permits repeating an activity for credit, there exists the problem of designing an evaluation system that presents a continuous challenge to those who are repeating, yet enables new students to compete for grades on equal terms with the experienced ones. For these reasons a graduated evaluation system should be employed in grading the Olympic lifts or the power lifts, whichever are used. Each of the practical evaluation tables, Tables 10.3 through 10.6, considers one type of lift, supplying appropriate grading criteria for three levels of performance which correspond to the number of times a student has taken the advanced course. For example, a student who is going through the course for the second time would be graded in accordance with Level 2 on each of the lifts. The data from which the norms for these tables were derived were collected from the records of more than 400 students enrolled in advanced weight training courses at Oregon State University.

The practical skill test is administered over two class periods (one lift each period) and is conducted as a regular AAU contest. This procedure provides the students with the experience of competition, which most have never had. For evaluating technique in the Olympic lifts, a

TABLE 10.3   Advanced Weight Training Proficiency Chart: SNATCH

Points*	20	16	12	8	4	2
Body Weight						
Level 1 (For those taking the course for the first time)						
123 and under	130	120	110	100	90	80
124–132	135	125	115	105	95	85
133–148	140	130	120	110	100	90
149–165	145	135	125	115	105	95
166–181	150	140	130	120	110	100
182–198	160	150	140	130	120	110
199–220	170	160	150	140	130	120
221 and over	180	170	160	150	140	130
Level 2 (For those taking the course for the second time)						
123 and under	140	130	120	110	100	90
124–132	145	135	125	115	105	95
133–148	150	140	130	120	110	100
149–165	155	145	135	125	115	105
166–181	165	155	145	135	125	115
182–198	175	165	155	145	135	125
199–220	185	175	165	155	145	135
221 and over	195	185	175	165	155	145
Level 3 (For those taking the course for the third time)						
123 and under	150	140	130	120	110	100
124–132	155	145	135	125	115	105
133–148	165	155	145	135	125	115
149–165	170	160	150	140	130	120
166–181	180	170	160	150	140	130
182–198	190	180	170	160	150	140
199–220	200	190	180	170	160	150
221 and over	210	200	190	180	170	160

* An additional point is given for every 5 pounds lifted over maximum.

scale of 0–15 points is used. A power snatch or clean, though each is a legal lift, requires very little skill compared to the split technique, hence would receive a very low score, 5 or fewer points. The instructor's evaluation points are added to those earned for the amount of weight lifted (see Tables 10.3 through 10.6), and the lift that yields the highest score on combined technique and strength is figured in the final total points column.

This grading system of evaluating combined skill and strength forces students to learn to rely on good technique and lift a reasonable amount of weight at the same time. Without this system some students would snatch light poundages to accumulate high technique points and then proceed to power snatch heavier poundages for strength points. Also, to encourage a student to extend himself to the limits of his ability, there is no established maximum as to the points that can be earned. For every five pounds lifted over the maximum listed in the tables, one additional point is earned.

TABLE 10.4 Advanced Weight Training Proficiency Chart: CLEAN AND JERK

Points*	20	16	12	8	4	2
Body Weight						
Level 1						
123 and under	175	165	155	145	135	125
124–132	185	175	165	155	145	135
133–148	195	185	175	165	155	145
149–165	205	195	185	175	165	155
166–181	215	205	195	185	175	165
182–198	225	215	205	195	185	175
199–220	235	225	215	205	195	185
221 and over	245	235	225	215	205	195
Level 2						
123 and under	190	180	170	160	150	140
124–132	200	190	180	170	160	150
133–148	210	200	190	180	170	160
149–165	220	210	200	190	180	170
166–181	230	220	210	200	190	180
182–198	240	230	220	210	200	190
199–220	250	240	230	220	210	200
221 and over	260	250	240	230	220	210
Level 3						
123 and under	205	195	185	175	165	155
124–132	215	205	195	185	175	165
133–148	225	215	205	195	185	175
149–165	235	225	215	205	195	185
166–181	245	235	225	215	205	195
182–198	255	245	235	225	215	205
199–220	265	255	245	235	225	215
221 and over	275	265	255	245	235	225

* An additional point is given for every 5 pounds lifted over maximum.

Examples 1 and 2 illustrate the grading procedure.

EXAMPLE 1. The student weights 165 pounds and is being evaluated at level one.

Snatch (Table V)	Weight Lifted	Technique Points	Strength Points	Total Score
1st lift	125	12	12	24
2nd lift	135	13	16	29
3rd lift	145	10	20	30*
Clean and Jerk (Table VI)				
1st lift	175	10	8	18
2nd lift	195	10	16	26
3rd lift	210	11	21	32*

* Total points of best lifts 62
Written examination (25 pts) 22
Final total points 84

TABLE 10.5   Advanced Weight Training Proficiency Chart: BENCH PRESS

Points*	20	16	12	8	4	2
Body Weight						
Level 1						
123 and under	180	170	160	150	140	130
124–132	195	185	175	165	155	145
133–148	210	200	190	180	170	160
149–165	225	215	205	195	185	175
166–181	240	230	220	210	200	190
182–198	255	245	235	225	215	205
199–220	270	260	250	240	230	220
221 and over	285	275	265	255	245	235
Level 2						
123 and under	195	185	175	165	155	145
124–132	210	195	185	175	165	155
133–148	225	215	205	195	185	175
149–165	240	230	220	210	200	190
166–181	255	245	235	225	215	205
182–198	270	260	250	240	230	220
199–220	285	275	265	255	245	235
221 and over	300	290	280	270	260	250
Level 3						
123 and under	210	200	190	180	170	160
124–132	225	215	205	195	185	175
133–148	240	230	220	210	200	190
149–165	255	245	235	225	215	205
166–181	270	260	250	240	230	220
182–198	285	275	265	255	245	235
199–220	300	290	280	270	260	250
221 and over	315	305	295	285	275	265

* An additional point is given for every 5 pounds lifted over maximum.

EXAMPLE 2.   The student weighs 180 pounds and is taking the course for the second time.

Snatch (Table V)				
1st lift	155	13	16	29
2nd lift	170	11	21	32
3rd lift	180	14	23	37*

Clean and Jerk (Table VI)				
1st lift	220	12	16	28
2nd lift	230	11	20	31*
3rd lift	failed	0	0	0

* Total points of best lifts 68
Written examination (25 pts) 24
Final total points 92

All final scores are placed on a curve for grade distribution.

TABLE 10.6   Advanced Weight Training Proficiency Chart: SQUAT

Points*	20	16	12	8	4	2
Body Weight						
Level 1						
123 and under	260	250	240	230	220	210
124–132	275	265	255	245	235	225
133–148	290	280	270	260	250	240
149–165	305	295	285	275	265	255
166–181	320	310	300	290	280	270
182–198	335	325	315	305	295	285
199–220	350	340	330	320	310	295
221 and over	365	355	345	335	325	315
Level 2						
123 and under	275	265	245	235	225	215
124–132	290	280	270	260	250	240
133–148	305	295	285	275	265	255
149–165	320	310	300	290	280	270
166–181	335	325	315	305	295	285
182–198	350	340	330	320	310	300
199–220	365	355	345	335	325	315
221 and over	380	370	360	350	340	330
Level 3						
123 and under	290	280	270	260	250	240
124–132	305	295	285	275	265	255
133–148	320	310	300	290	280	270
149–165	335	325	315	305	295	285
166–181	350	340	330	320	310	300
182–198	365	355	345	335	325	315
199–220	380	370	360	350	340	330
221 and over	395	385	375	365	355	345

* An additional point is given for every 5 pounds lifted over maximum.

appendixes

APPENDIX A: RULES FOR COMPETITIVE LIFTING

The following rules for conducting and judging a weightlifting meet were taken from the *Official AAU Rules Book.* A copy may be purchased by writing to the A.A.U. House, 3400 W. 68th Street, Indianapolis, Indiana 46268, and enclosing $2.00.

TECHNICAL RULES GOVERNING THE OLYMPIC LIFTS

Two-hands snatch

The bar shall be placed horizontally in front of the lifter's legs. It shall be gripped, palms downward, and pulled in a single movement from the ground to the full extent of both arms vertically above the head, while either "splitting" or bending the legs. The bar shall pass with a continuous movement along the body, of which no part other than the feet may touch the ground during the execution of the lift. The weight, which has been lifted, must be maintained in the final, motionless position, the arms and legs extended, the feet on the same line, until the referee's signal to replace the bar on the platform.

Important remark. The turning over of the wrist must not take place until the bar has passed the top of the lifter's head. The lifter may recover from either a split or a squat in his own time.

Incorrect movements in the snatch

1. Pulling from the hang.
2. Violent contact of the bar against the thighs.
3. Pause during the lifting of the bar.
4. Moving the hands along the bar during the lift.
5. Uneven extension of the arms.
6. Incomplete extension of the arms.
7. Finishing with a press-out.
8. Bending or extending the arms during the recovery.
9. Touching the ground with the knee or buttocks or any part of the body other than the feet.
10. Leaving the platform.
11. Replacing the bar on the platform before the referee's signal.

Two-hands clean and jerk

The bar shall be placed horizontally in front of the lifter's legs. It shall be gripped, palms downward, and brought in a single movement from the ground to the shoulders, while either "splitting" or bending the legs. The bar must not touch the chest before the final position; it shall rest on the clavicles, the chest, or on the arms fully bent. The feet shall be returned to the same line, legs straight, before performing the jerk. The lifter may make the recovery in his own time.

Bend the legs and extend them and the arms to bring the bar to the full stretch of the arms vertically extended. Return the feet to the same line, arms and legs extended, and await the referee's signal to replace the bar on the platform. After the clean and before the jerk, the lifter may assure the position of the bar. This means to withdraw his thumbs (or "unhook" if he has used this method in cleaning the bar) or to change the width of his grip.

Incorrect movements in the clean

1. Any unfinished attempt at pulling in which the bar has reached at least the height of the knees.
2. Pulling from the hang.
3. Violent contact of the bar against the thighs.
4. Touching the ground with the knee or buttocks or any part of the body other than the feet.
5. Cleaning in the squat position touching the knees or thighs with the elbows or upper arms.
6. Leaving the platform.

Incorrect movements in the jerk

1. Any apparent effort of jerking which is not complete.
2. Uneven extension of the arms.
3. Pause during the extension of the arms.
4. Bending and extending the arms during the recovery.
5. Leaving the platform.
6. Replacing the bar on the platform before the referee's signal.

POWER LIFTS

Bench press

The lifter may elect to assume one of the following two positions on the bench, which must be maintained during the lifts: (1) with head, trunk, and legs extended on the bench, knees locked, heels on the bench; (2) with head, trunk, including buttocks extended on the bench, feet flat on the floor.

The referee's signal shall indicate the time when the bar is absolutely motionless.

At the referee's signal, the bar is pressed vertically to straight arm's length, and held for two seconds. The lifter may use any method to bring the bar to the chest preparatory to the uplifting movement.

The spacing of the hands shall not exceed 32 inches measured between the forefingers.

Causes for disqualification

1. During the uplifting, any change of the elected lifting position.
2. Any raising of the lifter's head, shoulders, buttocks, or legs from the bench.
3. Any shifting of the same.
4. Bridging in any form.
5. Any heaving or bouncing of the bar from the chest.
6. Allowing the bar to sink excessively into the lifter's chest.
7. Any uneven extension of the arms.
8. Stopping of the bar during the press proper.
9. Any touching of the bar by the spotters before the referee's signal.
10. Failure to wait for the referee's signal.

Deep knee bend or squat

The lifter must assume an upright position with the bar across the shoulders in a horizontal position, not more than one inch below the top of the deltoids, hands gripping the bar, feet flat on the platform. (The use of a wedge at the heels, not to exceed 2 inches in height, is optional.) The bar is held motionless for 2 seconds. The referee's signal shall indicate the time. The spacing of the feet, which must be on the same line, is optional.

At the referee's signal, the lifter shall bend the knees and lower the body until the top levels of the thighs are below parallel with the platform. The lifter shall recover at will, without bouncing, to an upright position, knees locked, and hold for two seconds. The referee's signal shall indicate the time.

No part of the legs shall be covered except by a bona fide bandage of standard thickness.

The lifter may use any method to bring the bar to the shoulders preparatory to the lift.

Causes for disqualification

1. During the exercise, failure to wait for the referee's signal.
2. Any bouncing at point of recovery.
3. Any change of position of the hand on the bar.
4. More than one recovery attempt.
5. Failure to assume an upright position at start and completion of lift.
6. Any touching of the bar by the spotters before the referee's signal.
7. Any shifting of the feet during the performance of the lift.
8. Any shifting of the bar during the performance of the lift.

Two-hands dead lift

The bar must be laid horizontally in front of the lifter's feet, gripped with an optional grip with both hands, and uplifted with one continuous motion until the lifter is standing erect. At the completion of the lift, the knees must be locked and the shoulders thrust back. The referee's signal shall indicate the time when the bar is held motionless in the final position.

Causes for disqualification

1. Any stopping of the bar before it reaches the final position.
2. Failure to stand erect.
3. Failure to lock the knees.
4. Resting the bar on the thighs.
5. Lowering the bar before the referee's signal.
6. Any raising of the bar from the platform shall count as an attempt.
7. Any shifting of the feet during the performance of the lift.

WEIGHT CLASSES

For both Olympic and power lifting, bodyweights governing the classes
shall be:

Flyweight .... up to 114½ lbs
Bantamweight .... up to 123½
Featherweight .... up to 132¾
Lightweight .... up to 148¾
Middleweight .... up to 165¼
Lightheavyweight .... up to 181¾
Middleheavyweight .... up to 198¼
Heavyweight .... up to 242½
Superheavyweight .... over 242½

Weighing in of a competitor *must* take place one hour before the beginning of competition.

Lifters must be weighed nude.

If a competitor wears a belt, its width must not exceed four inches.

The use of grips or straps is forbidden.

Point scoring for meets other than national championship meets shall
be 5, 3, 1.

COMPETITION

1. The bar is loaded progressively, the lifter taking the lowest weight
   lifting first. In no case can the bar be reduced to a lighter weight
   when a lifter has performed a lift with the weight announced.

2. A lifter taking his first attempt must precede the lifters taking their
   second or third attempts with the same weight.

3. The poundage increases shall be 10 pounds between first and second
   attempts and 5 pounds for the third attempts. A lifter electing to increase the poundage by 5 pounds between the first and second attempts shall forfeit the third attempt.

4. In case of a tie, the lightest man at weigh-in shall be declared the
   winner.

APPENDIX B: THE HOFFMAN FORMULA

This table provides a fair means of comparing both individuals and teams
on the relative merits of their lifts. For each body weight between 110 and
210 pounds, a coefficient is given. Multiply the lifting total of a contestant
by the coefficient of his body weight to obtain his score. By this means,
one can compare the significance of the accomplishments of two men of
different body weights who lift different amounts. The table is especially
useful for scoring the efforts of two teams made up of men who are not
matched in body weight or the number of pounds they can lift.

Each lifter must be accurately weighed before competition begins. If his weight amounts to a fraction of a pound that falls short of one-half pound, it shall be recorded at the highest full pound; if the fraction exceeds one-half pound, his body weight shall be considered to be the next higher pound.

110	1.000										
111 -	.994	121 -	.935	131 -	.885	141 -	.840	151 -	.800		
112	.988	122	.930	132	.881	142	.836	152	.797		
113	.982	123	.925	133	.876	143	.832	153	.793		
114	.976	124	.920	134	.872	144	.828	154	.790		
115	.970	125	.915	135	.867	145	.824	155	.786		
116	.964	126	.910	136	.863	146	.820	156	.783		
117	.958	127	.905	137	.858	147	.816	157	.779		
118	.952	128	.900	138	.854	148	.812	158	.776		
119	.946	129	.895	139	.849	149	.808	159	.772		
120 -	.940	130 -	.890	140 -	.844	150 -	.804	160 -	.769		
161 -	.766	171 -	.736	181 -	.712	191 -	.692	201 -	.678	211 -	.668
162	.763	172	.734	182	.710	192	.691	202	.677	212 -	.667
163	.760	173	.731	183	.708	193	.689	203	.676	213 -	.666
164	.757	174	.729	184	.706	194	.688	204	.675		
165	.754	175	.726	185	.704	195	.686	205	.674		etc.
166	.751	176	.724	186	.702	196	.685	206	.673		
167	.748	177	.721	187	.700	197	.683	207	.672		
168	.745	178	.719	188	.698	198	.682	208	.671		
169	.742	179	.716	189	.696	199	.680	209	.670		
170 -	.739	180 -	.714	190 -	.694	200 -	.679	210 -	.669		

index